The Seven Concertos of Beethoven

Other titles by Antony Hopkins

Talking about Symphonies

Talking about Concertos

Talking about Sonatas

Music Face to Face (with André Previn)

Understanding Music

Sounds of the Orchestra

Pathway to Music

The Concertgoer's Companion

Beating Time (autobiography)

Downbeat Music Guide

Songs for Swinging Golfers

Musicamusings

Lucy and Peterkin

Music all around me

The Nine Symphonies of Beethoven

The Seven Concertos of
BEETHOVEN

Antony Hopkins

SCOLAR
PRESS

Published by
SCOLAR PRESS
Gower House
Croft Road
Aldershot
Hants GU11 3HR
England

Ashgate Publishing Company
Old Post Road
Brookfield
Vermont 05036–9704
USA

British Library Cataloguing-in-Publication data

Hopkins, Antony
  The seven concertos of Beethoven
  1. Beethoven, Ludwig van, 1770–1827 – Criticism and
  interpretation   2. Concertos – History and criticism
  3. Music – Germany – 19th century – History and criticism
  I. Title
  784.2'3'092

Library of Congress Cataloging-in-Publication data

Hopkins, Antony
  The seven concertos of Beethoven / Antony Hopkins
  ISBN 1–85928–245–8 (cloth)
  1. Beethoven, Ludwig van, 1770–1827.   Concertos.   I. Title.
MT130.B43H67   1996
784.2'3'092 – dc20   96–24729
                          CIP
                          MN

ISBN 1 85928 245 8

Typeset in 11 point Times by Raven Typesetters, Chester
and printed in Great Britain at the University Press, Cambridge.

Contents

Preface

We live in amazing times, times whose technological innovations we too easily take for granted. In the eighteenth century an extremely wealthy aristocrat would almost certainly have had a resident orchestra as part of his establishment; its members would even have been expected to travel to his summer palace for as long as it pleased him, as is proved by Haydn's 'Farewell' symphony in whose final pages is a subtle hint to his princely employer that it was more than time to return to Vienna. Today we do not have to incur the monstrous expense of such a household and even the wealthiest of us would not keep an orchestra. Why should we, when for a relatively modest price we can acquire a compact disc player and a collection of recordings? We may not own a palace or employ a horde of servants but we can command the presence of the world's greatest orchestras and the finest soloists to perform in our sitting-rooms whenever the mood takes us.

Admirable though such a state of affairs may be, there is a downside; too often music is simply regarded as a pleasant background noise to accompany our other activities. A composer of Beethoven's stature has more to offer than that, and it is my belief that the more detailed and thorough our listening, the greater our enjoyment will be. Concertgoers and record-buyers alike tend to pay more attention to the performer than to the work being performed. How often do we find ourselves drawn to a concert to hear a great soloist or conductor without bothering too much about what is being played?

It is the purpose of this book to counter such an attitude. The concertos of Beethoven are so well-known that we are in danger of no longer really listening to them. Certainly we can *hear* them, and while the family breakfasts and prepares for the day ahead, the radio may well provide a movement or two for our supposed delight. At least when we go to a concert we are hardly likely to eat our cereals and chatter while the orchestra play, even though it is assumed these days that recorded music is an essential when we dine at a restaurant.

Not everyone can read a musical score but I suggest that the ideal way to use this book is as a substitute for the printed music. By all means listen to the concertos; but as you do so, follow the commentary I have provided so as to focus your attention on Beethoven. If your understanding of his music is enhanced it will inevitably bring a greater love and enthusiasm in its wake. Music is a language of sorts, since language is a means of communication; the sound may be attractive but how much more worthwhile this communication is if we understand its significance. This book may be regarded as something of a musical tourist's guidebook, pointing out felicities and initiating us into the 'language'. If, in the end, you appreciate the beauty of these masterpieces even more, I shall not have failed for that is my sole intention.

A.H.
1996

Introduction:
The Concerto

All men are not born equal; even in the somewhat limited field of musical executants, some are endowed with infinitely greater natural ability than others. The concerto as a musical form is a logical reflection of the fact that in any group of musicians gathered under one roof, one or two will outshine the others in technical and musical ability. In the very early days, concertos tended to be for several players rather than one. There is a charming proof of why this was so in one of the Handel concerti grossi for strings; in the slow movement of the piece in question, there is a particularly elaborate ornament given to the solo quartet which at no time appears in the ordinary orchestral parts, for the simple reason that the rank-and-file players would have been unable to play it with the requisite neatness and agility. In other words, Handel had not conceived the form itself as something special; it was simply a composition for orchestra which reflected the superiority of the front-desk performers.

Vivaldi, who is said to have written upwards of 500 concertos, surely had talented individual players in mind; usually they were outstanding pupils at the Ospedale della Pieta in Venice, where for a long time he was in charge of the music. The concerts given there were a notable feature of Venetian life and were reputedly second to none.

Later, when Haydn arrived at Eisenstadt to take up his new post, he found only a tiny resident orchestra of about a dozen players. The first violin was a fine performer, an Italian called Luigi Tomasini, and it is small wonder that in the first symphonies that Haydn wrote for his new employer he frequently writes more virtuoso parts for a solo first violin and a solo second violin which he presumably played himself. The works may have been called symphonies but it was thus that his early concertos came about, and herein lies the explanation of the seemingly haphazard choice of instruments which composers so often appear to have made at the time.

The emergence of the soloist into the splendid isolation he came to occupy in the nineteenth century was a slow process. In the Bach concertos for violin or keyboard, the soloist usually plays with the orchestra at all times, establishing the tempo and generally acting as an orchestral 'leader'. Even in such a case as the slow movement of Bach's D minor keyboard concerto, where there is no indicated part for the right hand until the thirteenth bar, it seems certain that the harpsichordist would have played with the accompanying strings, perhaps directing them with an elegant wave of the right hand at times in order to show his complete command of the situation. Gradually the competence of orchestral players increased to such an extent that they could manage without the assistance of the soloist; remember though that the conductor as we know him today was still unknown in 1700. Reports tell us of such barbarous customs as the audible beating of time with a stick upon the floor, or with a roll of parchment on the lid of the harpsichord. Where direction was necessary it would almost invariably come from the keyboard player, but there seems to have been a remarkable absence of formality about musical proceedings, even in the complex world of opera. Johann Mattheson, who was not only a composer, harpsichordist, organist and singer, but a linguist, a dancer and skilled fencer as well, when singing a role in an opera, would periodically leave the stage and direct the music from the harpsichord in the pit. It was on 5 December 1704 that he found an obstinate young man called Handel at the keyboard who refused to give way, thereby provoking the challenge to a duel which is a well-authenticated incident in Handel's life. Honour was satisfied when Mattheson's foil, having easily penetrated Handel's guard, impaled itself on one of his waistcoat buttons. This story is not entirely irrelevant, since Handel was accustomed to delighting audiences at the opera-house by performing his keyboard concertos as interval music.

It was Mozart who established what we now think of as the classical concerto form. In essence what he did was to devise a grand sonata for soloist and orchestra, though there are certain differences between strict sonata form and the normal pattern of a Mozart concerto. What is the normal pattern? It is hard to say, since nearly every work of this kind has points of originality which make it an exception to any presupposed set of rules. For what it is worth, though, here is a rough ground-plan.

An orchestral exposition (known as the *tutti*, from the Italian word for *everybody* – meaning that all instruments are playing) presents us with most of the salient themes; but whereas in a sonata exposition the second subject will be in the so-called dominant key (a fifth higher than the tonic or 'home' key), in a concerto it is very much more likely to be kept in the original tonality. To make things more confusing, the composer will sometimes refuse to reveal the true second subject at all at this stage, preferring to save it up as a special treat for the soloist. (Beethoven and Mozart both have a lovable habit of fobbing us off with a 'dummy' second subject which, having been hailed with shrill cries of delight by the musical analyst, then fails to reappear until the recapitulation, much to our discomfiture.) On the whole, modulation to remote keys is avoided in the early stages, as this too is that much more effective if kept in reserve for a later moment. What distinguishes good concerto material from purely symphonic music is a very subtle suggestion that something is missing; that the music so far, although beautiful and satisfying enough in itself, has implications of potential decoration in the future. As the simplest possible instance I will quote a short passage from Beethoven's Third Piano Concerto. The orchestral part near the beginning reads:

Ex. Ia

but when this passage reappears some pages later, the pianist provides a nimble though admittedly not very significant decoration of arpeggios.

Ex. Ib

Experience teaches us to recognize such moments and to await expectantly the pleasures that lie ahead. In other words, we should not regard the orchestral exposition as something cut off from the main part of the movement, but rather as the framework of a plot into whose events the hero (or soloist) will duly move as chief protagonist. All the same, this orchestral introduction, or *tutti* as it is usually called, will often finish with a formal conclusion, terminating in a polite silence before the soloist plays a note. As composers became more adept at handling the form, the solo instrument's entry was managed with increasing subtlety.

With the soloist's appearance on the scene we have reached what might be termed a secondary exposition. Exceptions there may be, but as a general principle composers at this point will restate the opening material, this time including the soloist together with any additional comments he may care to make. In character this new statement is often much more akin to a development than an exposition, in that there is nothing to stop the composer journeying off into new episodes that have little or no relevance to what has gone before. One of the great excitements of concerto form is the element of fantasy it so often implies.

The line of demarcation between this secondary exposition and the development proper is a fine one, not always easy to perceive; all the same, there is a difference, and the introduction of new themes, excursions into more remote keys, even changes of tempo, are all more likely to occur in the true development section. Do not expect, however, such a concentration on the matter in hand as we find in the Mozart G minor symphony or Beethoven's fifth. In many concertos the development is an excuse for rhapsodic interludes; showers of notes may fly from the pianist's fingers, weaving delightful patterns that are in fact no more than decorative formulae of little thematic interest. If the themes are referred to, they are more likely to be found in the orchestral part, rather as though the orchestra was a crowd of anxious nannies trying to dissuade a capricious child from going too far on its own. Nevertheless, Beethoven's greatest inspirations often occur in the development, and it is usually at the moment immediately *before* the recapitulation that we find those passages whose harmonic tension (and consequently emotional intensity) are the greatest.

The recapitulation, once reached, will certainly begin with a restatement of the first subject, usually with a more co-operative attitude from the soloist than heretofore. But for the audience it is no time to sit back; the chance of new happenings at this point is far greater in a concerto than in a sonata or symphony. Not only is variety easier to achieve because of the contrast in colours between soloist and orchestra, but also there is always this element, already alluded to, of improvisation, of fantasy, which is an intrinsic part of the form. One thing we can be pretty sure of, though, is that at some point the soloist will drop out and allow the orchestra its head for a while. This convention is based on a purely practical reason in that it is designed to give the soloist a rest before he embarks on the most strenuous part of the movement, the cadenza.

The cadenza, rather despised by the purists, is for me one of the most fascinating attributes of the concerto. In the days of Bach, Mozart or Handel, and indeed right up to the time of Chopin or Liszt, the ability to improvise or make up music on the spur of the moment was expected from every musician. Matches were even held in which two performers would be sat down in turn at the keyboard and called upon to extemporize on a given theme. The cadenza gave an opportunity for the performer to display this skill, and while technical virtuosity was certainly called for, further development of the thematic material was as important. It is unlikely that truly improvised cadenzas were ever heard at public performances, since any sensible performer would presumably have prepared something in the process of learning the work. But the stimulus of an audience may well have provoked new flights of fancy, and most particularly the presence of other musicians in the surrounding orchestra would be likely to encourage the performer to new invention. What is undeniable is that the style of composition shown in those cadenzas by Mozart or Beethoven which have been written down is different from their usual manner. This is even true of the three-part keyboard fugue with which Bach's *Musical Offering* begins. It seems almost certain that this is a more or less exact transcription from memory of a piece that Bach had improvised on the spot to King Frederick. In it we find passages of free figuration that are quite un-fugal in character, as though Bach was doodling happily with his fingers while his brain was working out further possibilities of manipulating the fugue subject. Cadenzas, then, are the nearest thing we have to a recording of the great composers, for even if we make allowance for 'improvements' that may have crept in once the notes were put down on paper, it still seems likely that a cadenza by Mozart or Beethoven represents a reasonably honest transcription of what they would actually have improvised.

If the cadenza was a truly spontaneous invention, there had to be some indication to the orchestra that it was time they took up their instruments once again, and so it became established that a trill, or series of trills, was a signal to stand by. In due course the orchestra would enter with a triumphant affirmation of the first subject, whereupon (in nearly all of the Mozart concertos) the soloist would remain quiet till the end of the movement. It wasn't long before composers realized that the omission of the solo instrument from the final bars of a movement was a miscalculation, and Mozart himself, who thought of nearly everything – including serial music according to some wishful thinkers – experimented with the possibility of using the soloist right up to the end of a movement, as he did for instance in K. 491, the Concerto in C minor.

The second movement of the classical concerto is designed to show the poetic and lyrical qualities of the instrument. It is often the movement which displays the deepest feeling, but it is misleading to expect this in all concertos, as sometimes the composer may prefer to write what is virtually a song without words, a movement whose function is decorative rather than contemplative. As to the form of these movements, it is impossible to lay down any clear ruling. Some are variations, some are rondos, some are sonata movements. Form in slow movements is of less importance than it is in an opening allegro; there must be a shape that is satisfying to the listener, but the form is not essential to the actual drama as it so often is in a sonata movement. It is usually sufficient for us to sit back and wonder at the beauty of the ideas that are presented to us; we do not need to be so aware of structures and relationships.

The third and last movement (four-movement concertos are a rarity) is most usually a rondo, a form in which one tune appears a number of times with varying 'fillings' between the repetitions – a multi-decker sandwich in which the rondo-theme is the bread, and the layers of cheese, salami and lettuce are the intervening episodes. C.M. Girdlestone[1] has classified the one hundred and eleven finales of Mozart's maturity into seventy-six rondos, eighteen sonata-form movements and seventeen which are variations or minuets. Whatever the form, the function of the last movement is clearly to entertain; as in the symphony or the sonata, each movement serves a different purpose, the first to stimulate thought by elegant conversation about serious matters, the second to relax or edify, the third to delight and amuse. But there are exceptions to practically every statement that can be made about concertos, since of all large-scale musical forms it is the most flexible.

We come now to one of the most fascinating aspects of the growth of the piano concerto. If you want to buy a string instrument, and money is no object, you get one that is more than two hundred years old; there have been minor technical modifications to the violin, but basically it has remained unaltered. To buy a two-hundred-year-old piano with the intention of performing on it publicly would be the act of an unpractical eccentric; the instrument has changed out of all recognition and early examples are of more interest to the antiquarian or the musicologist. Aided by microphone and CD player, devotees of the so-called 'authentic' movement can make quite a convincing case for copies or reconstructions of early instruments, but however fascinating such exercises may be they pre-suppose that twentieth-century listeners can somehow acquire eighteenth-century ears. The tone of the early piano was dry and 'woody', it had little sustaining power, its compass was substantially less than that of the modern piano, its volume limited. The piano on which Mozart would have performed bore as little relationship to a modern concert grand as a 1900 Mercedes did to the sports racing car with which Stirling Moss won the Mille Miglia in 1955. This is a fact, but it is a fact from which we must draw the right conclusions. Mozart's scoring is wonderfully calculated in its balance between soloist and orchestra; whenever an important theme is given to the keyboard, the orchestra will either be silent or make sympathetic accompanying noises. On the other hand, many passages where the melodic interest lies in the woodwind or strings may be embellished by decorative cascades or notes from the piano, since there was no likelihood of their being obscured. It is these passages that are most liable to be distorted in modern performances; the dazzling technique and prodigious tone of the concert pianist of today causes figures to swamp the orchestra which Mozart or even Beethoven clearly intended to be no more than a silver lining. This is especially true in all too many gramophone recordings, where the already disturbed balance is made still more remote from Mozart's conception by artificial means. There is no need to deny ourselves the virtues of the modern piano when it comes to subtlety of touch, beauty of tone and sustaining power. But we must scale down its resources in sheer volume and brilliance, or we will get a totally false impression of the actual musical content of an eighteenth-century concerto.

In his first three piano concertos it is fairly clear that Beethoven had exactly the same problem to deal with as had Mozart. He rigs the balance in just the same way, never allowing the piano to compete openly with the orchestra. In the fourth concerto, which is the last truly classical concerto, the implied contest between soloist and orchestra is won by gentleness; this is most notably true of the slow movement in which the aggression of the orchestra is marvellously tamed by a constant turning of the other cheek, a refusal to fight which ultimately reduces the opponent to silence. Between the composition of his fourth and fifth piano concertos Beethoven apparently came into possession of a new piano. Despite his deafness he at once realized the potentialities of the instrument, and in the so-called 'Emperor' we see the result of his reassessment of the relationship between piano and orchestra. Here for the first time in musical history the piano stands up to the orchestra as an equal, even indulging in open defiance at times.

The popular appeal of the concerto, and the piano concerto in particular, is enormous. The reason for this is fairly obvious. To be a hero one must vanquish an outnumbering opposition. In the public eye, the soloist is a sort of hero, dominating the orchestra, and triumphing despite tremendous odds. An element of self-projection enters in, and the listener gets a vicarious thrill by imagining himself to be in the soloist's place. (Did he realize one-tenth of the work entailed in achieving the standard of performance which any concerto demands, he might think twice about it.) To the soloist, the concerto remains the ultimate challenge. There is little logic in this, since to play a solo sonata of the dimensions of the 'Hammerklavier' or the Liszt B minor would seem to be even more demanding. In the long run, it must be this very situation of 'one against all' that makes the concerto what it is, for every story needs a hero with whom the reader can identify himself. The hero in a concerto is just that much more obvious. . . .

This introduction is a modified version of the opening chapter of 'Talking about Concertos' (pub. Heinemann 1964) by the same author, now out of print.

Note

1. C.M. Girdlestone: *Mozart's Piano Concertos* (Cassell).

Piano Concerto No. 1 in
C Major, Op. 15

1 Flute, 2 Oboes, 2 Clarinets, 2 Bassoons, 2 Horns, 2 Trumpets,
Timpani, Strings.

It is hard to understand why publishers, having successfully
tackled the problem of renumbering the Dvořák symphonies,
persist in calling this piano concerto Number One when
Beethoven himself in a letter to Breitkopf and Härtel dated 22
April, 1801, makes it clear that it was written later than the
Concerto in B flat habitually called Number Two. Admittedly the
'Second' concerto was published later in a somewhat revised version, which explains the later opus number. Beethoven's words in
the letter refer to two other publishers:

> Hoffmeister is publishing one of my first concertos, which of course
> is not one of my best compositions. Mollo is also publishing a
> concerto *which was written later*, it is true, but which also is not
> one of my best compositions of that type.
>
> Trans. Emily Anderson, Vol. 1, page 53.

Beethoven's slightly dismissive remarks about the two concertos
are best explained by the fact that he was hoping to ingratiate himself with a rival publisher, and naturally wanted to give the impression that the best was still to come. Simple detective work with first
editions tells us that Hoffmeister published the concerto in B flat,
Op. 19, and that Mollo printed the one in C, here under discussion.
A quick glance at the score tells us at once that Beethoven

intended this to be a work of greater importance than its ill-starred predecessor for it demands five more players in the orchestra: two clarinets, two trumpets and timpani. Even so it begins quietly with strings only, and the full impact of his resources is reserved until bar 16 when there is a much reinforced version of the opening idea. It is in the character of a little march, whose most notable feature is a remarkably simple one, the jump of an octave.

Ex. 1a

This, as shown in bar 1, proves to be extremely susceptible to development, as Beethoven reveals later. (It is nearly always the case that in *allegro* movements he uses terse and succinct phrases greatly to his advantage; the Fifth Symphony is perhaps the supreme example.) The juxtaposition of loud and soft that is to be found in the B flat Concerto is here reversed and extended so that sixteen bars of quiet music is followed by forty bars as loud as he can make them. This louder section presents us with several subsidiary themes, of which one is of particular interest as it may be a seed from which a passage in the Fifth Concerto grew in Beethoven's mind.

Ex. 1b

The idea of the rising scale against a more sustained descent is certainly planted here; whether Beethoven was conscious of any resemblance between two widely separated works is a matter for conjecture.

The music stays resolutely in C major for an unusually long time, the one brush with the dominant (G major) being over almost before it has registered. However, the second subject, when it arrives after a dramatic silence, is in the very unconventional key of E flat major:

Ex. 1c

The woodwind have a bland response to this against which the violins have uneasy syncopations leading us to the even more unconventional F minor. The whole process is repeated, bringing us to G minor. At this point Beethoven begins a series of short modulatory phrases which take him nearer home with a hushed excursion to C minor. A link between the starting-point C and the unusual key of the second subject has at least been established for C minor and E flat major share a common key signature of three flats.

Will this offer Beethoven an easy way home to the tonic? No. The journey is deferred. The bassoon, hotly followed by the oboe, leads off with a reminder of the rising octave that began the piece. In no time we are plunged into a positive musical maelstrom with the full orchestra pitting the rising octaves against defiant scales which, after a visit to the sub-dominant (F major), land triumphantly on C major. The horns and oboes celebrate this with a joyous march that sounds as if Mozart had written it for Figaro; it is punctuated by a giggling phrase from the violins (which is deliberately trivial) as all the wind instruments, trumpets included, take up the march. After some perfunctory twirls we are reminded forcibly again of the importance of the rising octave from bar 1;

four times it is declaimed by wind or strings alternately. At last, with a rousing cadence confirming C major as the 'home' key this long introductory *tutti* comes to a close. At the entry of the soloist, Beethoven shows that he has learnt something from Mozart for he makes no attempt to contend with the orchestra; in fact the piano is almost apologetic so elementary are its first phrases, so lacking in display. Strangely enough this theme never appears later in the movement; its sole function seems to be to establish the individuality of the performer. Soon the orchestra gets back to basics with peremptory reminders of that all-important rising octave; this time it is greeted with cascades of arpeggios by the soloist. For the first time the pianist now takes notice of the octave, sometimes in the left hand, sometimes in the right, but it is never slavishly repetitive in his treatment and seems by turns a little angry or sardonic. In quite a short time the octave is given a new character by flowering into a melody which leads us via E flat major to stormy chromaticisms in G minor.

It is in the major of that key that the second subject now makes a gracious reappearance. (Mozart would probably not have revealed it so openly in the *tutti*, keeping it as a surprise until this moment; but Beethoven is still learning his craft and has other surprises of his own up his sleeve, as we shall hear in due course.) At first in the orchestra, but then in an increasingly florid version by the soloist, the theme is allowed to run its full course before flute and bassoon introduce a brief but tender motif whose repeated notes possibly bear a faint family relationship to the first bar of the work, although it is as remote as a second cousin twice removed.

Soon the soloist embarks on an athletic version of the 'Figaro' march, followed by a whirligig movement which transfers from the right to the left hand. Quite a little storm develops, with exciting chromatic triplets in the bass which later find their way into the upper part. There follows a wonderfully inventive passage, perhaps the most beautiful in the movement, in which the soloist initiates a long descent, modulating through a number of different keys before emerging satisfyingly into a drawn-out cadence based on Example 1b (page 12). A long trill signals the arrival at a centre-point of the movement and a quite substantial section for orchestra based at first on a contrapuntal treatment of the first bar; it is another example of Beethoven's ingenuity in developing such very basic ideas. After a considerable flurry of notes there is a silence, followed by a hushed reminder of the opening four notes – only this time they are based on G. Another silence. Tentatively the strings try the pattern a semitone higher on A flat. The full orchestra sees the possibilities in this and makes a huge unequivocal declaration that the future lies in E flat and no mistake.

The soloist responds with a long improvisatory passage based on an E flat arpeggio that would not be out of place in the Fifth Concerto. The music seems to shake off its classical restraint and becomes much more expansive. In no way a development of things that have gone before, it enables the soloist to establish complete independence. Further anticipation of the textures to be found in the Fifth Concerto appear in a passage where both hands move in parallel with chords an octave apart. The passage has a mature serenity about it quite different from the busy activity of nearly all of the rest of the movement.

Having allowed the soloist considerable freedom for some time, bassoon and then flute restore order with quiet reminders of the opening rising octave while the piano makes gruff comments in staccato unisons in triplets. The woodwind choir continues to develop the octave idea, disregarding the soloist, until an intriguing and mysterious section when the piano is given long, quiet descending chromatic scales that are not dissimilar to a passage in the recapitulation of the first movement of the Fifth Concerto. Indeed this work seems to contain the seed of the later one, nowhere more so than in a wonderfully hushed duet between piano and unison horns which strangely anticipates a passage near the end of the so-called 'Emperor' when the duet is between soloist and timpani. A slashing *glissando* in octaves, easy to execute on a light-touched piano of Beethoven's time but hard to bring off on a modern instrument, leads to what appears at first to be a conventional recapitulation for the full orchestra. It lasts precisely seven-and-a-half bars before the soloist takes over with a derivation of the rising scale which is part of the opening theme.

From now on the movement consists largely of transposed versions of material already heard. Re-acquaintance is made with the second subject, now in the 'home' key of C; we set our feet tapping to the 'Figaro' march; once more the whirling semiquavers lead to the chromatic 'storm', very much shortened; the long descending modulation through sundry keys catches our attention, as does the forceful repetition of the now familiar rising octave from the full orchestra. Powerful unisons in a previously unused dotted rhythm herald the arrival of the cadenza, which at the time Beethoven did not bother to write, leaving it to the inspiration of the moment.

Later he was to write no less than three cadenzas at different times, which suggests the inevitable dissatisfaction that is bound to occur when trying to graft something on to an earlier work when one's style has changed substantially with the years. What is unusual about his third cadenza (the one favoured by most pianists) is the absence of a final trill to warn the orchestra to take up their instruments again; the cadenza ends with two loud chords on the dominant seventh, a silence, a quiet and enquiring chord, an even longer silence (leaving the soloist's hands free to bring the orchestra in) and then a full version of the first six bars of the 'Figaro' march and four last allusions to the rising octave that bring the movement to a satisfying conclusion.

Unusually, piano and strings begin the slow movement together; the key is A flat whose third note, C, is imagined to be a pivot between the two scarcely related keys. The chord which is first given to the pianist is similarly spaced to the opening harmony of the Fourth Concerto, but it is a sound which Beethoven particularly associates with A flat major.[1] The Mozartean influence is particularly strong in this movement and there are some passages which could be mistaken for Mozart's, including one which is played unaccompanied in single notes, and, whether coincidentally or not, appears to be lifted out of the divine *Et incarnatus est* from Mozart's Mass in C minor.

The expressive initial phrases from the piano are taken still further by the orchestra before the pianist begins a decorative solo that is an exact copy of the sort of spacing we might find in a Mozart concerto; the accompaniment consists merely of occasional octaves while all our attention – and the composer's – is given to the right hand. The orchestra rather poignantly (but loudly) asserts E flat minor, before the *Et incarnatus* phrase is given to the piano, alternating with soft sighs on the woodwind.

The elaborate phrases which ensue are for the most part decorations of the E flat major chord or its close relatives, the texture remaining essentially Mozartean.

In due course there is a return to the opening theme, this time slightly elaborated. A brief passage for orchestra culminating in some strongly rhythmic exchanges leads to yet another reprise of the theme. Surprisingly it now has a positively waltz-like accompaniment which leads at times to some fascinating clashes between the 'twos' of the melody and the 'threes' that support them.

In the closing pages of the movement Beethoven establishes the clarinet as a notable partner to the pianist, and together they initiate a memorably beautiful coda which is perhaps the best part of the whole concerto. Certainly it is the section which manages most successfully to shake off the influence of Mozart; here, one feels, is the true voice of Beethoven, speaking to us maybe in the idiom of a dying century but making it his own.

It is the soloist who sets the final Rondo on its merry way with a theme whose ending is amusingly deferred three times; as might be expected, the whole orchestra take up the theme exuberantly, helped on its course by amusingly jarring notes in the bass; a rousing fanfare on horns and woodwind expresses general satisfaction, before the soloist has an energetic little passage which includes some entertaining hops and some lively arpeggios.

The orchestra are given the first presentation of the next episode to appear:

Ex. 1d

The soloist proceeds to mock this by putting the main notes after the beat, and then, with the help of the orchestra, shifting the tonality to E flat. An amusing duet follows in which the tune is divided between a low bass and a high treble; it involves some showy crossing of the hands since the central accompanying figure buzzes along happily without interruption. It passes through several keys before settling into G major, its arrival quietly endorsed by sustained harmonies on the strings.

Next the orchestra have a brief unison interlude in which mock angry phrases are interspersed with fleeting references to the main theme, slightly modified. Taking a cue from the local farmyard (remember that Beethoven loved the country) the pianist has some typically jokey and delightful impressions of clucking hens which, once exhausted, lead us back to the initial theme, presented without changes of any kind. Again it is repeated by the full orchestra, surprisingly without alteration or new direction.

The soloist now introduces a new theme in A minor with a positively samba-like rhythm, even though it is extremely unlikely that Beethoven ever heard any Latin-American music. As if to atone for this rather frivolous tune, it is immediately followed by a somewhat academic passage of counterpoint which the woodwind are happy to copy. Beethoven appears to have been particularly taken with his 'samba', for he repeats it three times in all. He then pays a return visit to the farmyard with the hen-clucking theme.[2]

By now Beethoven has exhausted the material he needs for this particular movement; nearly everything is a reworking of themes we have already heard. This is not to say that he cannot still surprise us. A brief cadenza leads to a lengthy trill which diverts the music into the alien key of B major, in which new tonality the initial rondo theme now appears. For a time things seem to hang fire; then the safe return to C major, the 'home' key is greeted joyously by the full orchestra. A delightful dialogue ensues between the soloist and different sections of the woodwind; it consists of deliberately naïve scales and fragments of the theme. In childlike mood, the pianist introduces a last novelty in the shape of a tune we have not heard before, then teases us with the first three notes of the rondo. For a moment the horns and oboe pretend to be serious with a sudden slowing of the tempo; then in a raucous six bars the full orchestra brings this vastly entertaining movement to an end.

In this chapter I have tried to convey something of the irrepressible humour of this finale. It is important to remember that this is the music of a high-spirited young man, and that what we now call 'classical' music had not then acquired the sort of aura with which we now tend to regard it. Music can be fun without being funny; but in this movement there are moments of such sheer delight that the proper response, if not outright laughter, is most certainly an inward chuckle. I am sure that the first to lead the way, and none more pleased to do so, would have been Beethoven himself.

Notes

1. See especially the sonatas Op. 26, Op. 110 and the slow movement of Op. 13.
2. In case my suggestion seems too irreverent, it is only fair to point out that descriptive pieces were much in vogue at the time; furthermore there were good precedents in earlier times – for example Rameau wrote a delightfully vivid piece called *La poule* as well as many others of a picturesque nature, while his great near-contemporary François Couperin attached a descriptive title to many of his compositions. If Beethoven's music here does not suggest a hen then it must represent an attack of the hiccups, which is every bit as irreverent a thought!

Piano Concerto No. 2 in B Flat Major, Op 19

1 Flute, 2 Oboes, 2 Bassoons, 2 Horns, Strings.

In 1795, when he would have been twenty-four and was just starting to be known as a promising young composer rather than as a brilliant pianist, Beethoven was commissioned to write a concerto for a concert to be given to raise money for the widows and orphans of the Society of Musicians in Vienna. (He had attempted a concerto before in 1784, a concerto in E flat, Op. WoO 4, but only a solo part and a reduction of the orchestral part for a second piano survives. It is very much in the style of one of his predecessors J.C. Bach, and cannot be regarded as particularly worthy or characteristic.) We do not know if any money changed hands in this case, but it is quite probable that Beethoven felt it was a significant occasion that would bring him useful publicity; at that stage none of his work was published, and he may well have felt that if he made a sufficient splash with the new work it would be a useful *entrée* to the publishing world; it was probably to be his first public appearance although he had of course played often in the salons of the aristocracy. He started writing enthusiastically but, as is often the case, insufficient time had been allowed, and by 27 March, two days before the concert date, the finale had still not been written. It was at this point that Beethoven went down with a severe dose of colic — abdominal pains were to trouble him throughout his adult life. Forced to take to his bed, doctor by his side, Beethoven pressed on with the last movement, handing it out page by page to no less than four copyists in the next room. A set of orchestral parts was essential, and in the days before photo-copying all duplicated string parts had to be individually hand-copied.

Beethoven's troubles were not over for when he arrived at the hall to rehearse on the day (presumably feeling none too well), he found to his dismay that the piano was half a tone flat. Woodwind and brass could not tune down to its pitch and so there was nothing for it – Beethoven would have to transpose. Thus it was that the first performance of this new concerto, which Beethoven had certainly had no time to practise, was given with him playing it in B major instead of the proper key of B flat. One cannot imagine a modern pianist agreeing even to attempt such a feat and it is small wonder that Beethoven put the work aside as an unhappy memory, only issuing it in a somewhat revised version three years later and after he had written what is now known as his First Concerto.

Any young man can scarcely be blamed for taking models, and since Mozart might be said to have mastered the keyboard concerto as a musical form it was to Mozart that Beethoven turned, not in person of course but as a spiritual ancestor. A formula often used by Mozart (and for that matter a number of eighteenth-century composers) was an alternation between quasi-heroic ideas that established the tonic or 'home' key and more gentle responses. Beethoven unashamedly copies his predecessors in this respect, and the concerto begins with the full orchestra loudly declaiming the notes that comprise the chord of B flat major:

Ex. 2a

The response which is given to strings only is gently placatory:

Ex. 2b

The gestures are next duplicated in the dominant, laying down a significant pattern. The violins now introduce a substantially new theme whose lyrical turn of phrase suggests to ears unaccustomed to the conventions of classical music that it might even be a premature second subject.

Ex. 2c

Example 2a now returns, no longer in its initially bold guise but quietly merry. It devolves into an urgent but suppressed duet between violins and cellos which is developed quite stormily until it reaches a loud formal cadence in F minor and three unmistakable unison C's spread over three octaves.

There is a silence, followed by the interpolation of three very quiet D flats as though the orchestra can scarcely believe what the young Beethoven has put in front of them. A new theme appears; is this perhaps destined to be the second subject?

Ex. 2d

Apart from its unexpected key (D flat) there is something else worth mentioning about this theme. Beethoven clearly wanted the first phrase to be on the second violins only and the gently curving response to come from the firsts. However his practical knowledge caused him to doubt whether the seconds would be confident enough to present this important new idea on their own. Thus it is that the first bar is scored for all the violins, only thereafter to become a dialogue between seconds and firsts as was originally intended.

Cellos and basses spread an air of gloom with a faintly sinister phrase in B flat minor, derived from Example 2d but utterly changing its mood. They are answered by the upper woodwind who give the impression that they don't really know where this is all leading to. It is the violins who begin a step by step climb back to the first theme, now accompanied by an urgent tremolo which conveys a new excitement; perhaps the soloist is about to make an entrance. The moment is not quite yet however, and the violins get quite carried away in response to the new mood of urgency, extending the opening idea through several keys (C minor, E flat major, F minor) until the original B flat major is quite forcibly restored. Cellos, basses and violas play an active part in confirming this safe arrival at the 'home' key, and then, rather surprisingly, we hear again Example 2c, now admitting its importance but clearly not the second subject. The exposition ends with two loud chords affirming B flat major. How will the soloist enter after this long and thematically rich introduction?

When at last the soloist enters the fray it is in a manner that Beethoven had clearly learnt from Mozart; no attempt is made to dominate or rival the orchestra in any way. Rather it is with a completely new theme that remains the exclusive property of the soloist. What is un-Mozartean is that it begins on a high F, the highest note on the keyboard of the time. (It raises the question how did he begin in that nightmarish first performance when he was forced to transpose? Since there was no high F sharp, did he play the passage an octave lower, or was this a modification of the original, introduced by him in his subsequent revisions?) By starting in this area he chose the thinnest and most delicate tones that were available on his piano as if to underline that his conception of the concerto was not to attempt a trial of strength with the orchestra. These first phrases gradually descend from the heights culminating in a resounding cadence in B flat, both hands now playing in the bass clef.

The ensuing orchestral phrase is particularly interesting for its curious foretaste of the Fourth Concerto. Indeed, were it not for the matter of key it might well be confused with an extract from the later work. A glance at the passage will confirm what I mean, though it is only with hindsight that we see the relationship.

Ex. 2e

I doubt if Beethoven realised the ultimate use to which he would put this pattern; at any rate it only appears once. It is disregarded by the pianist who now embarks on an extension of the very opening theme, introducing athletic leaps with stamping harmonies in the bass; a four-octave scale of C major ushers the orchestra into the proper key of F major and the true second subject which, with another trick learned from Mozart's example, has not been divulged up to now. A rather Mozartean phrase it proves to be, beautifully scored:

Ex. 2f

The pianist takes this up at a higher octave, adding a few decorations of his own. A lengthy trill leads to an inspired little section in D flat major, matching but not duplicating the comparable D flat passage in the orchestral introduction. Some scales, trivial at first, lead to quite a storm, with whirling semiquavers modulating swiftly through a number of keys; soon there is an exchange of interests and a similar figure is given to the left hand. (The thought of Beethoven having to transpose this particular passage surpasses belief; all the fingerings he may have had in mind when he wrote it would have had to be totally changed.) Three loud cadences for full orchestra elicit a soft answer that indeed 'turneth away wrath'; they are followed by a cadenza of sorts which is built on the dominant and which cleverly suggests that it is slowing down to a halt before picking up speed again and leading in to a sixteen-bar passage for full orchestra. Here the listener must not be beguiled into listening to the violins and the apparently new material they present; it is down in the bass that the real melodic substance occurs, with important references to the very first bar of the piece.

An interesting suggestion of a recapitulation follows in which Beethoven starts with the piano solo exactly as it was when it first entered except that the material is now in the dominant key of F major. A brief excursion into G minor involving strings and piano leads to three strident unison D's which give way to the 'surprise' note E flat which again suggests a certain amount of incredulity from the orchestra. Not surprisingly the orchestra continue as they did before, but this time the pianist snatches the tune from them after a mere four bars. Soon a dialogue develops between a brand new motif based on repeated notes in the woodwind and discreet arpeggios from the pianist (they are specifically marked *p*). In turn, the pianist extends the repeated note motif in a passage rather suggestive of part of the last movement of the 'Moonlight' sonata (Op. 27, No. 2). For a while the pianist keeps us in suspense until a rapid scale brings us to the recapitulation proper. It is in a considerably condensed form in which the soloist is involved much sooner than before. The second subject appears in its rightful place this time, but everything is recognisably derived from what has gone before and the attentive listener should have no difficulty in hearing the relevance of each passage.

Beethoven left space for a cadenza but failed at the time to write one, no doubt happy to leave it to the inspiration of the moment. When he provided one (presumably by request) at a much later date he failed to match the style adequately and produced something which, if not exactly 'a monstrous carbuncle', does rather stand out like the proverbial sore thumb.

The slow movement, if not directly influenced by Mozart, could be regarded as the sort of music he might well have written if he had lived to be fifty – an extension of his idiom rather than a direct copy. The texture is seldom more dense than Mozart's, the writing a little more adventurous.

Ex. 2g

The orchestral opening sets a very slow tempo, a real adagio, and it might almost be taken from a religious work.

However, the ensuing two-octave scales in the first violins suggest a somewhat less sacred atmosphere and it is not long before the piano is summoned by a peremptory rhythm on loud unison B flats. The opening theme is played twice by the soloist, the second time an octave higher and with increasingly elaborate decorations. Brief phrases are tenderly exchanged between orchestra and soloist before the theme appears yet again, in even more elaborate guise and encompassing over four octaves between the hands at times; one feels that the ghost of Mozart has been firmly laid, all the more so as the pianist begins a strangely rippling figure as accompaniment to a woodwind reprise of the theme. (Although far from strict, the movement is in effect in variation form.)

The exchanges between orchestra and soloist reappear before an interesting passage for piano alone which introduces a new texture with fourths in the right hand, single notes in the left; it modulates through several keys until increasingly powerful trills lead to quite a disturbed passage for orchestra in the minor, starting as a variation on the theme but soon breaking free and preparing the way for the most inspired page in the movement. It is a cadenza of sorts, but as far from the expected virtuoso display as can be imagined. In single notes, unaccompanied, it is marked *p* and *con gran espressione*. Hushed strings remind us of the opening phrases of the movement, interleaved with these expressive utterances. Finally the movement is brought to rest by the orchestra alone; one feels that the soloist is reduced to silence by the emotion so clearly and yet so reticently expressed.

Beethoven begins the last movement with eight bars of solo piano, presumably so that he could set both tempo and mood for the orchestra. The theme is joyous, even a little frivolous, and if this is the same music that he penned hastily from his sick-bed it says a lot for the power of the mind over physical frailty. The orchestra repeat the theme boisterously, and then become serious for a moment with a phrase that twice inspires a shower of broken octaves from the pianist. Soon the soloist introduces a new tune with a rustic air:

Ex. 2h

The orchestra seem to mock this with a somewhat grotesque version, Beethoven's way of making the 'wrong-note' joke that
composers use so often when they are feeling satirical. A swift
interchange between orchestra and pianist leads to a Scarlatti-like
passage in which the soloist continually widens the gap in the right
hand by degrees from a third to a tenth. Part of the fun lies in the
fact that each attempt to reach the top note is doomed to failure, the
pianist invariably brushing the note immediately below. (Were
these musical hiccups perhaps inspired by the fit of colic
Beethoven was enduring at the time?) A few random scale-like
passages suggest that the pianist has momentarily lost the way, but
salvation comes with another repetition of the rondo theme. The
orchestra redirect it to G minor, leading to a delightfully syncopated episode:

Ex. 2i

The woodwind try in vain to inject a note of sobriety into the
proceedings but the high-jinks of the piano part prove to be irrepressible.

We have now heard the bulk of the material in a concerto that
never presents a real challenge to the listener, though more than
enough to the soloist. There is a brief new tune in E flat over a busy
but conventional left hand, but it is not significant and soon disap-
pears in a welter of runs. The rustic tune bounces back, now in the
tonic key of B flat, and then once again the pianist appears to lose
all confidence, with two enquiring phrases separated by a silence.

This leads to a delightful joke in which Beethoven not only goes
suddenly into the 'wrong' key, G major, but also shifts the accent
of the rondo theme so that what was once in the rhythm of
'*Hump*ty *Dump*ty *sat on a wall*' becomes '*Hump*tee **Dump**tee sat
ON a wall'. The orchestra restores order with a return to the proper
key of B flat and re-establishes the original accentuation. We have

reached the coda at this point; the orchestra has a more respectable version of the syncopations that were such a notable feature of Example 2i, while the pianist practises arpeggios to delightful effect. A long descent in chromatic thirds leads to a brief exchange in which the phrase given to the piano hops while the answer given to the orchestra glides. A naïve little tune dissolves into more hiccups before Beethoven's last joke; the music seems to recede into near-total silence, broken only by very quiet isolated chords from the piano. Entering into the mood the orchestra has two equally hushed chords; then, as though with a roar of laughter from Beethoven who loved playing practical jokes of this kind, they wind up the movement with a sudden *ff*.

Historically, the impression we have of Beethoven is usually one of a rather solemn, severe character. Nothing could do more to dispel that image than this movement, bubbling over with musical high spirits and humour from start to finish.

Piano Concerto No. 3 in C Minor, Op. 37

2 Flutes, 2 Oboes, 2 Clarinets, 2 Bassoons, 2 Horns, 2 Trumpets, Timpani, Strings.

In this concerto Beethoven might be said to have 'come of age' as a composer of works for soloist and orchestra. Although there are still traces of the Mozartean influence (he was known to play the C minor and D minor concertos of Mozart as favourite works), and although sketches of the first three concertos show him to have had all three in mind at the same time, he shows a new mastery of material and a far greater individuality in all aspects. It is perhaps symbolic that it had largely been written in 1800 since it faces the new century boldly and appears to reject the past in a way that the previous two did not. The work is essentially forward-looking, and might be said to have laid the foundations on which the great romantic concertos of the nineteenth century were ultimately to be built.

Insight into his strange method of working is provided by a young musician called Seyfried who turned the pages for him at the first performance. (The habit of playing from memory is credited to Liszt and would have been regarded as exceptionally eccentric at the time.) Normally, when a composer writes a concerto for piano, one would expect the solo part to be worked out and written more or less in full, and the orchestral part as the less important except for the occasional *tutti*, to be merely sketched but not filled in in detail, at least in the first draft. With a performance in mind, orchestration would of course have to be completed onto a full score so that a set of parts could be made, but right from the first the solo part would have been there, even if a little amplified in the intervening time. When we read Seyfried's account we realise how unusual was Beethoven's way of working:

> At the performance of his Third Concerto, he asked me to turn the pages for him; but – heaven help me! – that was easier said than done. I saw almost nothing but empty sheets. At the most on one page or the other a few wholly unintelligible signs that could as well have been Egyptian hieroglyphics, scribbled down to serve as clues for him. He played nearly all of the solo part from memory, not having had time to put it all on paper. He gave me a secret glance whenever he was at the end of one of the invisible passages, and my scarcely concealed anxiety not to miss the decisive moment amused him greatly, and he laughed heartily at the jovial supper which we ate afterwards.

At first Seyfried must have thought his task would be fairly easy since the orchestral introduction at the beginning of the work is the most substantial of any of the concertos; it is truly symphonic in range. It begins with little indication of storms ahead; unison strings are entrusted with an important theme, although at this stage it is given out quite quietly without the least suggestion of ostentation:

Ex. 3a

There is little enough of this as it stands, but even so we need to regard bars 2 and 3 as separate entities when Beethoven comes to develop them. It is a theme which emphasises the importance of the tonic 'C' and the dominant 'G', and they need to be borne in mind throughout the first movement. The woodwind respond with an identically shaped phrase but based on dominant harmonies. The violins next introduce a new melody, perhaps derived from bar 2, but spreading its wings with a lovely rise of an octave. It tends to make us less aware of the rising figure in the bass which is a cleverly stretched version of the first three notes; it could be said then that this new development is in fact a fusion of bars 1 and 2, skilfully contrived to look like new material. There follows a succinct exchange between strings and wind (Example Ia in the Introduction) which should arouse our suspicions that there is something missing – a piano part! Suddenly the violins, and soon the full orchestra, break into a much extended version of the initial theme, now in the relative major (E flat) and no longer restrained but positively triumphant. A strongly syncopated theme emerges with a bass that moves in contrary motion, rising by even paces while the top line falls. At this stage it is in E flat minor but if transposed into the 'home' key of C minor it is seen to be a possible development of bar two:

Ex. 3b

Whether this relationship was intended by Beethoven or not we shall never know; the subconscious works in strange ways, and it may be that the idea of a phrase falling through five notes was implanted so deeply in his mind that it reappeared in this form without his realising.

The woodwind calm things down after this stridency, making way for the second subject. It is in E flat major, the closely related key that shares a key signature (three flats) with the tonic key of C minor. Here Beethoven departs from the Mozartean precedent of holding back the true second subject until it can be disclosed by the soloist; this is no dummy designed to deceive but the real thing:

Ex. 3c

Surprisingly it is repeated in C major by the woodwind gracefully accompanied by strings. A slightly sinister passage (strings *tremolando*) leads to an interesting reappearance of the opening theme, interesting because it too seems at first to be in C major, but turns out, however, to be in the sub-dominant, F minor. To a layman this would appear to be only of theoretical interest; to Beethoven it is considerably more than that, and is indeed the sort of musical punning which makes the language of music so fascinating.[1]

Rather plaintively the woodwind introduce a new tune beginning with a four times repeated note:

Ex. 3d

Another contrary motion idea appears briefly, and then accompanied by a shudder on the upper strings the cellos and basses remind us several times of the drumbeat rhythm we originally heard as early as bar 3. The *tutti* ends with a powerful version of the initial theme and three crashingly loud C's played by the entire orchestra.

Now according to Mozart's convention, such a loud ending to an introduction would inevitably lead to an almost diffident entry from the solo piano, since no purpose could usefully be served by attempting to compete with the orchestra; what is more, the pianist would have been given a previously unheard theme that could be regarded as uniquely confined to the piano. Beethoven will have none of this: three scales, uncompromisingly marked *forte*, lead to the opening theme in octaves, both hands, a statement of a boldness that so far as I know had never been known before. In order to make absolutely sure of his intentions, Beethoven not only repeats the *forte* injunction but even adds a *sf* (strong accent) on the top of the phrase. The ensuing match to the woodwind response is marked a contrasting *piano* (soft) before the soloist embarks on a free variation on the original orchestral part of bars 9–16.

There follows the little interchange between orchestra and piano which is briefly quoted in Example 1b. It modulates successfully to the relative major (E flat), in which key the orchestra sternly reminds us of the first theme. The pianist is unimpressed, and after two passages which are frankly nothing but showing off, embarks on an expressive variation of Example 3b. This soon becomes increasingly elaborate, with difficult leaps in the bass which graphically demonstrate the agility of Beethoven's left hand.

After a gradual unwinding, the second subject appears in the piano part, almost unaccompanied and without embellishment. The orchestra quietly copies, only for the pianist to have a delightful flight of fancy whose descending decorations emulate happy chuckles. For a moment or two there is a discussion of the theme shown as Example 3d, which leads us surprisingly into the alien key of G flat. There follows a passage which could indeed have been written by Mozart in so far as it is based on segments of the scale in either hand and on split octaves in the upper part where needed. A long trill (under which clarinets and horns present a triumphant version of the first theme) and a rushing scale downwards lead to a quite substantial orchestral passage based for the most part on familiar elements; the only new departure is a gloriously broken scale in the violins, based on the rhythm of the third bar.

Beethoven begins his Development ingeniously with three D major scales on the piano obviously referring back to the original entry, but in this unexpected key; it leads not immediately to the first theme but to a version of bar 3. This is quietly echoed by flute and oboe and then slightly distorted by a plangent bassoon. The strings in unison have a further reminder of this all-important rhythm, and lead us gently to the key of G minor. An expressive episode follows in which the pianist in simple octaves muses on the first subject, gently nudged onwards by the cellos with yet more reminders of that rhythm. Sliding effortlessly into flowing triplets the piano part soon offers a decorative accompaniment to the woodwind, who extend the opening three notes in various ways. A couple of waspish trills show the pianist to be getting tired of this subsidiary role, and a shower of broken octaves follows, until a rapid downward scale encourages the orchestra to give out theme one in a tremendous unison.

It is easy to fall into the trap of imagining this to be the start of a normal Recapitulation, and there is always the risk of sitting back and saying 'I've heard all this before'. That is precisely what Beethoven hopes, for straight away he has surprises in store, starting with the loud response from the woodwind, no longer the meek souls they were originally but positively blaring out their version of the theme. There follows a touching little dialogue between orchestra and piano which consists of hushed reminders of the motto rhythm (bar 3), and pleading little phrases from the soloist.

In due course the second subject reappears, now in the tonic (C major); indeed, despite surprises, this proves to be the Recapitulation, and all the events of the next few pages will be familiar, even though in different keys from their initial appearance. Beethoven, as might be expected, leaves space for a cadenza, which no doubt caused Seyfried total panic as it would have been improvised on the spot. In fact it was nine years before Beethoven bothered to write one down, and it is now the one usually played, although there are others in existence. What Beethoven did do, though, was to devise a wonderfully novel way of finishing the movement after the cadenza. Here he makes magical use of quiet timpani repeating the motto theme from bar 3. Veiled descending arpeggios from the pianist give a positively nocturnal effect until an increasingly urgent little pattern leads to a tremendous outburst from the orchestra. A torrent of downward arpeggios in C minor leads to four ascending scales which are surely related to the entry of the pianist in the first place. Powerful unison C's bring the movement to an end, a moment that poor Seyfried must have greeted with some relief. Surely in the next movement he would be able to relax.

A considerable surprise awaits us. Even today the choice of key, E major, comes as a shock; admittedly a similar contrast is to be found in one of the Haydn sonatas, but it is an unusual key to follow C minor, for the unison C's which end the first movement with such a positive affirmation of tonality do not exist within the scale of E major. The first chord is, then, a contradiction of all that has gone before, for it is a key that has appeared at no point in the first movement, not even as a brief moment in a modulating passage. It can be explained if we regard the sixth note of the C minor scale (A flat) as changed chromatically to G sharp, the same note on the piano but with vastly different harmonic implications. It is interesting to compare the opening of the slow movement of an adolescent sonata with the opening of this movement, the one so like Mozart in texture and melody, the other as unmistakably Beethoven with its sonority so profound even by his standards; yet the melody is almost identical even though the notation is different:

Ex. 3e

(originally in F major)

The piano begins the movement, setting a tempo for the orchestra, an extremely slow genuine six in a bar. The theme contains a striking modulation into the key of G major in the ninth bar, and this meditation is notable for two further points. One is a strange *tremolando* effect to be found in the left hand which would not surprise us in Liszt but is unusual in Beethoven; the other is the fact that this quite lengthy solo at the beginning of the slow movement is unique to this concerto. In all the other concertos of Beethoven it is the orchestra that sets the mood with an introduction that may only be brief, but which is always significant.

The orchestra gives a muted response to this solo, which we at first assume is going to be a straightforward variation but which soon proves to have a life of its own. It is worth noticing that the cellos and basses are given separate parts here instead of their normal unanimity; it makes for a particularly rich texture, but one which a modern cello section must beware of making too weighty. Soon they combine in an expressive descent while the violins have an increasingly florid line which, with assistance from the woodwind, folds tidily but firmly away in an E major cadence.

An elaborate solo in thirds ensues, of the type that was to become more and more favoured as the cult of the keyboard virtuoso developed; it certainly anticipates a texture beloved of Chopin, and indeed the writing might be seen as a halfway mark between Mozart and the mid-nineteenth century composers. Whether Beethoven intended this passage to be a variation on the opening theme is open to speculation; certainly there is a sort of 'family resemblance' which, with a bit of wishful thinking, can make it seem like one, but it is rather too distant from the theme for a first variation – if indeed it is one. It is more likely that the theme had exerted so powerful an influence on Beethoven's subconscious that he inevitably produced something which seems like a variation without actually being so.

The writing for the piano grows increasingly elaborate as a short colloquy with the orchestra leads to a cadence in the dominant (B major). Ingeniously the orchestra then modulate to G major, thus matching the modulation of which the solo piano has given us a foretaste in the opening presentation of the main theme.

A strange section follows at the centre of the movement; it is like an operatic duet, with flute and bassoon playing the parts of soprano and baritone. It sounds not unlike Schumann in his more classical *persona*, with rippling arpeggios in the piano part which emphasise the chamber music quality of the music. This is terminated by a long descending scale starting from a high A that was still unattainable on many of the pianos extant in Beethoven's day. After covering four octaves in its descent it leads to a reprise of the opening theme, this time shared between orchestra and soloist. As might be expected, the pianist's contribution is rather more elaborate, covering a wider range and considerably embellished. Beethoven again divides his cellos and basses in the ensuing orchestral passage, but once they are reunited, the pianist supports their expressive line with some wonderfully effective scales. Soon there is a brief cadenza, in single notes, marked like the one in a similar place in the second concerto, '*con gran espressione*'. Horns reiterate a low E in octaves as the piano, with a few poignant harmonies, brings this profoundly expressive movement to rest, only to have a last surprise for us as the full orchestra plays a loud chord specifically marked *fortissimo*. It is probably a trick he learned from Haydn who often ends his slow movements thus, literally indicating that it is the end of the movement and that the audience might applaud. The near silence broken by a few apologetic coughs with which we greet such a moment nowadays would have been considered a mark of disapproval. Beethoven came to resent the interruption caused by applause and cleverly thought of effecting a link between his slow movement and finale ·in the Fifth Concerto, thus foiling those impatient souls wishing to clap.

The function of this final E major chord becomes clear musically when we realise that Beethoven has effected an exact reversal of the enharmonic link that justified the choice of E major in the first place. If A flat can be said to 'equal' G sharp in the crossover from the first movement to the second, then obviously G sharp can 'equal' A flat in the transition from the second to third movements. So it is that the second actual note of the movement (falling on the first beat and therefore slightly accented) is an A flat. The transition is more acceptable to the ear than the eye as

the pianist begins this Rondo movement; it is a robust tune more
suited to country folk than to the aristocracy.

Ex. 3f

The woodwind repeat this against a running counterpoint,
although Beethoven marks their contribution *p* in case they should
seem too raucous too soon. The soloist proposes a second limb to
the tune, which seems momentarily to slow down, indulge in a
brief cadenza, before whisking happily back to the matter in hand.
The full orchestra proceeds to take up this second part enthusiastically. For a brief moment oboe and flute even flirt with the major
over repeated G's from the violins, but Beethoven realises that it is
a little early for such a radical departure, and he quickly and forcefully reasserts the minor. A brief fanfare salutes this triumphant
return, but the pianist has other ideas and after briefly agreeing to
it, playfully modulates into the *relative* major (E flat) and produces
a delightfully skipping tune that we have not heard before. It contains, after its initial descent, a rising phrase of which a more
sophisticated version is to be found in the Fourth Concerto. To
make a comparison easier I have transposed the example from the
later work down a third so that it now appears to be in the same
key; this is not 'rigging the evidence', as some might think, since
the principle of a chromatic rise with a running left hand is the
same in both cases (see Example 3g).

The tune is taken over joyfully by violins and flute, eliciting a
clatter of triplet semiquavers from the pianist which sound like the
musical equivalent of peals of laughter. A few Scarlatti-like leaps
of two octaves merely add to the fun, before the strings adopt a
more sober note by introducing yet another element in smooth

Ex. 3g

counterpoint. Indeed, after the high spirits of what has gone before it seems positively academic. Such propriety does not last for long however and the pianist soon embarks on a busy extension of the dominant (G major) culminating in a huge chromatic run. It leads us to the 'surprise-which-is-not-a-total-surprise' – the long-awaited return of the initial theme. We have known that its return was inevitable since the movement is a Rondo, but Beethoven has been so lavish with new ideas so far that we are not to know pre-cisely when that return will be.

A new and slightly longer cadenza (written out by Beethoven) interrupts its progress, ending with an upward run which has been a hazard for conductors ever since, as they stand poised to bring the orchestra in at exactly the right split-second.

It is the clarinetist who introduces the next episode, a melliflu-ous tune that is quite a contrast to the slightly angular main theme. The soloist seizes on it happily, and for some time a little duet is sustained between the two instruments. Beethoven puts a restrain-ing hand on their enjoyment by initiating a little fugue (*fugato*) based on the initial theme. It strikes a severe academic note which, however, should not be taken too seriously. As it develops, its opening three notes are picked out in the woodwind in a series of false entries, eager to start the subject but not allowed to. Soon even the trumpets join in with a mock-serious fanfare. Their strident reiterated G's are taken over by the remainder of the orchestra, appearing for the moment to be bogged down. In a semitonal rise that perhaps harks back to the Second Concerto and looks ahead to the Violin Concerto, they move very positively to the adjacent A flat. The pianist accepts the note enthusiastically but then appears not to be quite sure what to do with it. It is at this point that Beethoven has a delightful musical pun in which he again makes play with the equation that A flat equals G sharp. In a move that exactly parallels the shift from C minor to E major that was so surprising between the first and second movements, he subtly changes the tonality and quietly introduces a somewhat romanticised version of the original theme. The violins, as if slightly puzzled by this development, softly repeat the E, and then, unconvinced, try out a speculative F; it is again a rise of a semitone, matching the one that came before. Tentatively the cellos and then violas remind us of the opening three notes, suggesting that it is high time we got back not only to the theme but to the proper key. Their pleadings do not go unheeded, and soon there is a concentrated reprise of most of the material we have heard before.

For a time Beethoven toys with the main theme, first giving it to the piano in D flat, then using its opening notes to modulate briefly through various keys, E flat minor, F minor, until at last he effects a safe return to C minor, and pauses expectantly for a cadenza.

This proves to be an eminently suitable theme for the 'Grand Old Duke of York', for it 'marches up to the top of a hill and marches down again'. The descent is a little more fraught than the ascent and leads to four teasing attempts to establish the dominant (G) again. It is a joke he had clearly much enjoyed making at the start of the last movement of the First Symphony, and which he repeats here to similar effect.

Delighting in the surprise, the pianist suggests that it is time we all went into the major, and embarks on a witty and scintillating Coda. It is based on five slightly altered opening notes, but any previous hint of even mock severity is discarded. High spirits prevail, and Beethoven even introduces a new tune, slightly syncopated, which dances on its way to a happy conclusion. Beethoven liked to refer to his moments of good humour as his 'unbuttoned' mood, and here he truly seems to have relaxed. After the rather sombre opening of this concerto and the profound feelings expressed so eloquently in the slow movement, it is good that the clouds finally disperse in these eminently enjoyable final pages.

Note

1. To put it simply 'C' in C minor is the basic note of the scale; in F minor it is the fifth, and therefore has a different function.

Piano Concerto No. 4 in G Major, Op 58

1 Flute, 2 Oboes, 2 Clarinets, 2 Bassoons, 2 Horns, Strings.

It is hard for us today to appreciate the full impact that this work must have had on the listeners at its first performance in March 1807. (Tovey gives 22 December 1808, but later authorities suggest the earlier date.) Imagine the scene; there is a feeling of excitement in the house as the audience awaits the arrival of Beethoven to play his latest concerto. Already he is accepted as a creative genius, albeit an eccentric one whose platform behaviour can be unpredictable. A Beethoven première is always an occasion for the Viennese, and they are full of anticipation as he takes his place at the piano to play and presumably direct the new work. The whispered chatter dies down; how will he begin the convention of an orchestral introduction – mysteriously, perhaps, on cellos and basses or with a blare of brass and timpani? And then this extraordinary and unprecedented happening makes all present catch their breath; it is the *soloist* who begins, and not even with a masterful cascade of notes but with a soft and gentle phrase that is far from what they expect (See Example 4a):

Those who are now familiar with this unique beginning love it for its beauty; but the original element of surprise is inevitably harder to appreciate. The surprise we *can* appreciate is the orchestral response to the soloist's opening phrase. In the remote and unforeseen key of B major it is gentleness itself. The subtlest of

45

Ex. 4a

modulations takes us back via D major to the home key of G, there to start the real exposition. At first this takes the form of a duet between violins and cellos. Occasional clashes such as G sharp against G natural add spice to the harmony, but essentially the next few bars establish both the importance of G major as the 'tonic' and of the repeated-note theme first proposed by the pianist.

It has been suggested that this may have a more than coincidental resemblance to the motto theme of the Fifth Symphony on which Beethoven was also working sporadically at the same time. It was his custom to have several works in his mind simultaneously and the sketches for both appear to coincide. However, repeated-note themes occur so frequently in his music that too much should not be made of this; if there is a connection between this and another work it is more than likely to have been with the so-called Second Concerto, where there is a passage immediately after the first piano entry which remarkably anticipates this idea and to which Beethoven may have taken a fancy, thinking it should be developed further. (See p. 25, Example 2e.)

The orchestral exposition is particularly rich in themes and the one that appears next might be taken for the second subject were it not for its unconventional key of A minor. Led off by the first violins it is soon answered by an oboe, cunningly modulating from C major to B minor. A third phrase is offered by first violins and flute, this time going from G major to F sharp major – actually the dominant of B minor. Each phrase elicits a brief, quiet but almost military comment plucked out by cellos and basses; but it is the frequent transitions from key to key that give the music its forward impetus and raise the question in our minds, 'When and how is the soloist going to come in?' The strings, marked *sempre pp* (always very soft), remind us of the opening and then build a substantial climax that triumphantly re-establishes the tonic key of G major with this memorable phrase:

Ex. 4b

This, scored for full orchestra, has a galvanising effect on the lower strings who embark on a passage of considerable activity before everyone comes to a halt on the sub-dominant harmony of C major followed by the dominant, D major. A sudden diminuendo leads to a change of mood in which semiquavers are still to be found but in part-scale formation instead of aggressive and jagged. This is taken up briefly but quite angrily by the lower strings who break off sharply on an E flat, leading us to expect yet another modulation. 'No you don't' says Beethoven, and with a beneficent chord on the woodwind leads us back to the home territory of G major. Gently woodwind and then strings remind us of the very beginning, thus bringing this substantial exposition to a close.

But does it? If this work (like the Haydn symphonies) were to be given a nickname it might well be the 'Unexpected'. Over and over again throughout this first movement Beethoven exploits the element of surprise. Surprise number one was the opening with the solo piano; number two was the soft orchestral entry in the 'wrong' key of B major. Now we have an orchestral exposition which ends on an extreme dissonance:

four times repeated and marked *forte* for the full orchestra. This impatient gesture is completely disregarded by the soloist, who now enters unobtrusively with an unprepared unison that is strangely at odds with the orchestra's offering. They have implied, despite the G in the bass, a dominant seventh – D, F sharp, A, C, D; the soloist 'ought' to come in at least on one of the strong notes of this chord, D, F sharp or A. Instead, the pianist quietly enters on the weak note C, following it with an F sharp and then another C in a higher octave. Together these notes suggest a curiously bleak harmony, contradicting the warmth and tenderness of the very first chord of the concerto. The passage is ingeniously contrived to gives an impression of acceleration, going from duplets to triplets, and from triplets to semiquavers and then sextuplets, packing more and more notes to the beat as though the soloist was gathering strength for the considerable task ahead. A double trill leads to a more contemplative passage in sixths before there is a short development of the initial theme which the soloist quickly diverts into a rapid display of athletic semiquaver triplets. (These and other similar passages dictate a leisurely tempo for the movement as a whole.) Meanwhile the orchestra seem to remind the wayward pianist of the matter in hand by offering gentle quotations of fragments of the opening theme. It is to no avail; soon the soloist embarks on a positively Chopinesque improvisation in the very top register of the keyboard. It is in the previously unheralded key of B flat and reduces the orchestra to quiet supportive chords which to the keen analyst might be regarded as an augmentation of the main theme but are more probably just cushions of harmony. Soon more rapid triplets are to be heard before a down-and-back-again scale, covering no less than five octaves, leads to the true second subject which Beethoven has cunningly kept secret until this moment. Quietly stated by strings alone it is in the 'proper' key of the dominant (D major) which up to now, strangely, he has managed to avoid.

Ex. 4c

Even this theme only flirts with the dominant briefly, for after three bars it drifts into B minor. It is instantly repeated, divided between bassoon and clarinet while the soloist adds a curiously dissonant descant which in slow motion sounds more like Bartók than Beethoven. (E sharp against F sharp, D sharp against E natural, etc.) The original marking '*dolce*' (sweetly) suggests that even Beethoven thought that this might be 'going a bit far'. Perhaps on a period piano the dissonances merely added a touch of spice to the harmony instead of the rather acid and spiky effect achieved by most modern pianists.

Soon we are led back to the familiar material of the Exposition by means of a couple of sustained trills accompanied by brilliant arpeggios and some glittering passagework in both hands. The music is treated in an interesting way here. Bars 29–58 were originally for orchestra only; now they are almost exactly duplicated (although transposed) as bars 134–164, the significant difference being the very decorative part the pianist plays from bar 141 onwards. Particularly effective in a variation introduced by the soloist which begins in C major:

Ex. 4d

Meanwhile the oboe happily plays the little march it originally had as part of the exposition (bars 33–36). Inevitably semiquavers become triplet semiquavers as the orchestra heads towards Example 4b which appears now to be in two moods, the first bar accompanied by thunderous arpeggios, the second on tranquil woodwind. Chromatic scales and a long sustained double trill lead to a magical moment when the soloist reiterates the theme high up in D major; but it is only a moment, for in two bars there is a crescendo from a dreamy *p* to a loud *ff* – one of only six occasions in the whole of the first movement when that normally characteristic marking appears. (The reticence of the solo part is remarkable when compared to the Fifth Concerto.) Perhaps realising that the frail tones of the piano of his period could not dominate a full orchestra Beethoven now allows the orchestra to take over with a suitably transposed version of what originally appeared as bars 54–72. Instead of finishing on the strident dissonance shown on page 47 he allows the soloist to interrupt with a totally unexpected note; the orchestra have left a chord of D major hanging in mid-air, and the F natural that now gently intrudes on it is a complete contradiction that makes a strong impression without pianistic fireworks.

It leads to one of the most beautiful and mysterious passages in the movement. Four times the soloist reiterates softly descending chords divided between the hands and each time leading to a different destination. This figure is then taken over by the first violins although there is a tendency nowadays for over-enthusiastic pianists to drown them by drawing too much attention to the accompanying, but surely less important, arpeggios. Meantime the bassoon and oboe or flute take turns in offering variants derived from the very opening theme. At last the soloist breaks free, first with glittering triplets and then with a strong rhythmic pattern pounded out between the hands. Cascading arpeggios covering nearly five octaves at a time and a huge chromatic run lead, via some trills, to an unexpected new development. Marked very soft and sweetly (*pp dolce*), the pianist introduces a brand-new theme based, one might almost think, on a child's five-finger exercise. Charming though it is we should not disregard the mutterings of the cellos and basses beneath, who keep reminding us of the rhythm of the original theme. More insistent in their reminders are various woodwind instruments and even the horns, before the soloist, in skittish mood, introduces yet another idea based on a rising scale enlivened by dancing syncopations and gurgling trills. A sustained and oft-repeated dominant seventh leads through several massive chords to the Recapitulation, one of the only occasions (if not the only one) when the soloist dares a trial of strength with the orchestra. The concerto began with a piano solo and it is only right that the Recapitulation should do likewise. The opening theme is now elaborately decorated, but although it starts *ff* with that declamatory gesture, within four bars the original mood of gentleness is restored. The orchestral reply, still in the unexpected key of B major, is now accompanied by shimmering triplets.

For some time the music follows its initial course, but the piano provides a sudden diversion into E flat major in which key Beethoven gives us a comparable but more elaborate equivalent to the Chopinesque 'improvisation' that appeared earlier. It is not an exact variation but its function is the same – to provide a brief respite from more Classically controlled material by its essential Romanticism.

The orchestra again introduces the second subject, now in the tonic key of G major, and the piano again supplies its dissonant little descant. Allowing for the necessary transpositions the Recapitulation pursues a conventional course until the cadenza. Presumably Beethoven did not have the time or perhaps the inclination to write this, and he left a blank. Later, probably at the request of several players, he provided us with a considerable cadenza which shows a curiously uneven mixture of the inspired and the workaday. Since then, somewhat dissatisfied with Beethoven's attempts, a number of people have tried their hand at writing one, the most notable (despite its rather over-romantic flavour) being by Clara Schumann. However it was Beethoven who supplied the sublime and again unexpected re-entry of the orchestra. According to convention the cadenza should finish with a long trill on A (to wake the orchestra up as some cynics might think), resolving on G to coincide with the orchestra's loud affirmation of that key. Here Beethoven specified the trill on A, but instead of resolving it he merges imperceptibly into a lyrical, almost nostalgic version for the piano of Example 4b – the very phrase which it had enunciated a few bars before the cadenza. A last fond look at the opening theme leads to a torrent of scales and the end of a movement notable throughout for its lyrical and expressive quality.

The movement that now follows is perhaps the most original of all the slow movements from the concertos; certainly the conception is almost unique though César Franck was to copy it blatantly in his *Symphonic Variations*. Liszt described it as 'Orpheus taming the Furies', and it may be that Beethoven had some such idea in mind. Basically it consists of a dialogue in which the orchestra (strings only) is gradually reduced to silence by a pianist who, from the first, consistently remains aloof and unmoved by their initially abrupt and angry manner. However I have an alternative interpretation to Liszt's which may have some validity. In 1802 Beethoven wrote an extraordinary letter (now known as 'The Heiligenstadt Testament') in which he bared his soul to his brother in a most uncharacteristic way. Emphasising the misery of his deafness he frequently uses words such as 'isolation' and 'solitude'. Is it not possible that this movement symbolizes his isolation and withdrawal from the material world, which beats in vain about his now unhearing ears? Only when the orchestra has been reduced to silence does the pianist (i.e. Beethoven) allow himself to grieve openly in phrases whose emotional expressiveness is in striking contrast to the reticence of what has gone before.

The movement starts with loud unison strings playing an abrupt phrase whose dotted rhythm is eminently classical and might well come from a Handel cantata. The pianist replies with a chorale-like phrase whose serenity is in complete contrast; indeed one wonders if 'reply' is the right word, so detached does he appear to be. Is the pianist, in this case actually Beethoven, playing not to the orchestra but to himself? Again the strings declaim their angry theme, this time modulating to D major instead of staying, as they formerly had, in E minor. It's as if they are saying 'Why won't you take any notice of us?' Again the pianist pursues a solitary course, seemingly oblivious and unmoved. Gradually the orchestral phrases are both truncated and reduced in volume until at last they are down to a single *pizzicato* note. It is at this point that for the first time the pianist is allowed the openly expressive phrases I mentioned earlier; it is as though a door is closed on the orchestra, and, alone at last, the soloist is permitted an untrammelled expression of grief which good manners had previously forbidden. '*Forgive me then, if you see me shrink away when I would fain*

mingle among you ... All alone ... I must live like an exile.' (the
Heiligenstadt Testament.)

Three trills lead to an extraordinary passage as eloquent of the
'wringing of hands' as anything Beethoven ever wrote. A brief
cadenza (for right hand only) leads to a cadence in E minor;
cellos and basses mutter a memory, no more, of the opening
theme, and this amazing movement ends with a sigh.

As if from a great distance we hear the strains of a crisp little
march, though more for Oberon's fairy retinue than the brigade of
guards. The soloist instantly embroiders the first phrase in a somewhat frivolous mood, as the little bubbling trills indicate. The
change of mood from deep despair to sheer delight could scarcely
be more extreme. The following phrase is rather smoother in out-
line but it too is echoed by the pianist. The concept of alternation
established in the slow movement is still maintained but where formerly the soloist stayed aloof, now the joke (for joke it clearly is)
is shared. Suddenly the full orchestra bursts out with a reprise of
the march theme, now somewhat extended by a passage that is
notable for the broken octaves which give it a curious angularity,
disguising its scale-like derivation.

Ex. 4e

This is tossed between soloist and orchestra in a delightful manner
until the soloist embarks with some determination on a passage
that could easily be taken for a gruelling exercise from Czerny at
his most ferocious. Modulating through several keys it ultimately
arrives back at the key from which it started, A, though now we
should regard the A as the dominant of D.

The figuration changes from semiquavers to triplets and as the
music calms we sense the arrival of a new theme, a sublime tune
which Beethoven marks with a sustained unchanging pedal

throughout – an effect which is acceptable on a period piano but which muddies the texture overmuch on a modern one.

Ex. 4f

p dolce

This is much to the orchestra's liking and is taken up in a lovely burst of counterpoint that is a highspot of the movement. As if distracted by the beauty of this, the pianist establishes a less lyrical mood with a flurry of arpeggios which ultimately lead, via an amazingly rapid chromatic scale, to an orchestral reprise of the opening march. A more or less exact recapitulation follows until a series of modulations leads us away into regions unexplored up until now in the movement. Frantic arpeggios in E flat or B flat minor are interspersed with lively quotations in the woodwind of fragments of the original tune. These continue for some time, even allowing the pianist to relax a little into triplets. Nowhere is the concept of Development better exemplified than here, for Beethoven sticks to the rhythms of the opening march while completely transforming them.

In due course the lyrical tune at Example 4f is reached, though not before an extraordinary passage in which the two hands seem considerably at odds with each other. Once again the lyrical beauty of a contrapuntal section for orchestra is countered by athletic arpeggios from the pianist, who for a while is stuck in E flat as the violas play a lovely extension of the opening march theme, now transformed into a positive serenade.

After sundry orchestral musings upon fragments of the theme, accompanied by unison arpeggios in a high register, the orchestra displays a certain impatience by playing *ff* a distorted version of the opening march, and modulating to C major – the dominant of which key (F, B, D) is seized by the soloist and extended through four octaves. The music dissolves into a short and hushed cadenza and once more a rapid chromatic run leads to a reprise of the march tune. This time it is given to the pianist in an ingeniously disguised version before the orchestra enthusiastically confirms its safe arrival. Beethoven cannot resist taking an affectionate final glance at Example 4f after skilfully sidestepping into first F sharp major and then into C. Four times its opening phrase is passed through the orchestra against increasingly insistent scales from the pianist.

The cadenza which follows must be short according to Beethoven's instructions (*la cadenza sia corta*) and ends in a flurry of trills. The music calms with beautiful and nostalgic versions of the march theme to which the piano adds delicately spicy decorations which gradually have a soporific effect. Just as the music threatens to come to a complete halt Beethoven appears to say 'This won't do', and launches into a final *presto*. Reiterations of dominant sevenths become ever more clamorous until the orchestra explodes into one last version of the march theme, now so much quicker that one senses a considerable anxiety on Beethoven's part to 'get the thing over with'. He hastily dismantles the last few notes of the theme, splitting them between piano and orchestra. Then, with a few arpeggios and a perfunctory *Amen*, he ends this, surely the most lyrical of the five piano concertos.

Piano Concerto No. 5 in
E Flat Major, Op. 73

2 Flutes, 2 Oboes, 2 Clarinets, 2 Bassoons, 2 Horns, 2 Trumpets,
Timpani, Strings.

To call this work 'The Emperor' as is the custom is singu-
larly inappropriate, unless it is to consider it as an Emperor
among concertos. At the time of its composition the most
notable Emperor in Europe was Napoleon, and in 1809 his armies
first besieged and then occupied Vienna. During the bombardment
of the city walls, legend has it that poor Beethoven would take
shelter in his brother's cellar with pillows or cushions clasped to
his ears lest the noise should further damage what was left of his
gravely defective hearing. The occupation was from 13 May to 20
September, a harrowing six months for the Viennese; food was
short owing to the demands of the French troops, and every house-
holder had to pay over considerable sums, calculated according to
the freehold or the rental value of their homes. Despite these priva-
tions, Beethoven continued to work; some of his energies were
devoted to mundane tasks such as selecting and copying exercises
in theory which he drew from the works of Fux, Albrechtsberger
and others for the benefit of his favoured pupil the Archduke
Rudolph. He regarded the Archduke with great affection, and it is
to him that not only the famous 'Farewell' Sonata (*Les Adieux* Op.
81a) is dedicated, but also this very concerto. As was his way,
Beethoven had been mulling over it for some time, but certainly

the finishing touches were applied in that miserable summer. Napoleon's invasion however was not the only problem with which he had to contend.

In the autumn of the previous year (1808) he had taken lodgings at the house of his friend and patron the Countess Marie Erdödy. (It is curious how Beethoven managed to reconcile his aversion to the aristocracy as a matter of principle with his dependence on them as a matter of reality.) In the spring of 1809, when the Napoleonic armies were not far away, he discovered that his manservant was receiving a handsome supplement to the no doubt miserable wage that Beethoven paid him, and from the hand of none other than the Countess herself. Instantly he jumped to the unworthy conclusion that this money was in payment for sexual favours, not realising that this was evidence of her kindness in trying to ensure that for once Beethoven would be able to keep the same servant for some time. (He normally behaved so eccentrically that they left after a month or two, finding him to be an impossible employer.) Hence it is that we find on the sketches of this same concerto such remarks as 'What more can you want? You have taken the *servant* instead of the *master* ... What a substitution!!!! What a wonderful exchange!!!! ... You wanted a servant, now you have one.'[1]

The assumption that the Countess was gratifying her sexual appetite with the servant proved to be completely unfounded, but to save further embarrassment Beethoven moved to rooms in the Walfischgasse. It may have been a fit of self-loathing that caused him to choose a house that he knew also housed a brothel but we shall never know! Perhaps his extraordinary jealousy may even suggest that he had had (or hoped to have) a sexual relationship with the Countess himself, but there is no other evidence to support such a conclusion. It is not really likely.

With such distractions to occupy his mind it is surprising that Beethoven was able to produce the final version of the concerto. The first performance was given in the following year, 1810, by which time a set of orchestral parts could have been made, but publication did not materialise until February, 1811. According to some contemporary accounts it was received with ovations but this was not always so. At another performance in

Vienna the concerto was indifferently received and a writer of the time tells us why:

> If this composition, which formed the concerto which had been announced, failed to receive the applause which it deserved, the reason is to be sought partly in the subjective character of the work, partly in the subjective nature of the listeners. Beethoven, full of proud confidence in himself, never writes for the multitude; he demands understanding and feeling, and because of the intentional difficulties, he can receive these only at the hands of the knowing, a majority of whom is not to be found on such occasions.[2]

Since then it has become one of the most frequently performed of all the Beethoven keyboard concertos and is as well-known by its nickname as the Moonlight Sonata, incidentally a sobriquet of which Beethoven would have disapproved every bit as much.

The key of E Flat is established beyond all possible doubt at the start of the concerto. Like footmen at some grand occasion proclaiming the arriving guests' names, the orchestra gives out in a stentorian voice the three chords in the order Tonic, Sub-dominant, Dominant, the last-named being somewhat corrupted by the addition of its seventh (the fourth note of the E flat scale) in order to facilitate an easy return to the tonic. Each of these three 'announcements' is followed by a virtuoso flourish by the soloist, flourishes which increase in length and complexity each time as if to demonstrate the importance and supremacy of the piano. This was an entirely new development for which the instrument-makers must take some of the credit. It was a time of constant develop-ment in wind, brass and keyboard instruments, and in spite of his deafness (by then severe) Beethoven realised that a new piano which had come his way was for the first time capable of dominat-ing the orchestra. It was for this reason that the opening of the concerto is so radically different from that of its predecessors; one feels that the three mini-cadenzas or flourishes are a sort of celebration. At last, they seem to say, we pianists no longer have to court the orchestra; we are the masters now and they must bend to our will.

However, in Beethoven's hands the orchestra does not have to play as secondary a role as it does in some later concertos such as those by Schumann or Chopin, for there now follows a substantial *tutti* in which the main themes are presented in positively symphonic terms. This 'exposition' is unusual in that it never really departs from the tonic key of E flat; a brief visit to E flat minor does not represent a significant enough drift away from 'home', and this pull towards E flat is so strong that any wanderings towards other keys are swiftly called to order.

The first to appear, and rightfully so since it is the most significant of all the themes, is a somewhat military affair, initially on the strings, but later repeated by the woodwind choir:

Ex. 5a

As though the point has not been made sufficiently clear, the fundamentals of the E flat tonality are hammered home by brass and strings alternately:

coming to rest on the dominant (B flat). A slightly syncopated fragment follows:

with a considerable amount of movement in the lower parts, and off-beat reinforcement in the woodwind and horns. A violin flurry takes us into E flat minor, in which key we find a strangely muted march:

(d)

pp   *etc.*

which, in the terms of a sonata-form movement, turns out to be the true second subject. Mozart usually kept it in reserve for the soloist to reveal at a later point, so this may be regarded to a certain extent as a departure from tradition. On the other hand the theme is not at all like the conventional idea of a second subject; normally one would expect it to be in the dominant (B flat) which it is not, and it completely lacks the lyrical character which one associates with such supportive themes. The horns at least put it into the more acceptable key of E flat *major* and impart a smoothness which it had lacked before. The opening theme is not far away though, as anxious mutterings in violins and cellos tell us; soon the full orchestra takes up the thread with much emphasis on the rhythm of bar 1 of Example 5a, lifting it gradually through more than an octave until they reach a high E flat in considerable triumph. The woodwind introduce a calming influence with a delightful but brief motif based on four-note portions of a descending scale:

(e)

p

which leads to the important passage in contrary motion shown in Example 1b. Further loud affirmations of E flat major, endorsed by repeated notes at full volume by the trumpets, ensure that we get the flavour of the key; tonality was still an important and essential part of the composer's conception, and Beethoven is truly concerned throughout this exposition that he should establish the 'home' or tonic key in our minds.[3] The violins then have a brief lyrical moment:

(g)

p   *etc.*

faintly disturbed by mutterings of the all-pervasive rhythm in the bass. And then, against a background of repeated quavers in the wind, the soloist makes a long-awaited reappearance. It is a strange entrance, almost as though wishing not to be noticed, but giving an opportunity to loosen the fingers with a chromatic run of over three octaves, culminating in a long trill that commands silence from the orchestra.

Given the chance to develop the theme in a more individual style, the pianist at first treats it almost as a chorale with quiet four-note chords in both hands before a springing motif rises through more than an octave, only to descend in triplet chords and then rise again in ever quicker notes to a satisfying climax. For a mere four bars the orchestra takes over, with horns and trumpets pounding out the notes that comprise the tonic chord, and strings replying equally strongly with the sub-dominant (A flat). The soloist changes the mood in an instant, with a gently rocking figure which at first echoes the orchestral phrase (but putting it into the minor) and then moves smoothly into G flat major. At this point it is the bassoon which becomes the focus of interest, playing the theme (c) rather less strenuously than on its first appearance in the orchestral exposition, and accompanied almost chatteringly by the piano. Soon the orchestra is silenced as the pianist unleashes a torrent of semiquavers; are they in G major or B minor? We are poised between the two keys for a time until the question is resolved by the reappearance of the second subject, (d) unusually marked *pp* (very soft), and with a minimal accompaniment on plucked strings. The sun seems to come out as the music relaxes into C flat major; it is a key we normally recognise as B major, but for reasons of admittedly academic convenience Beethoven prefers to call it C flat. Notice the subtlety of Beethoven's scoring here, with clarinet and bassoon gently sustaining harmonies a tenth apart, and a single cello holding a quiet G flat in the bass. This seems to be altogether too sentimental for the orchestra; the mood changes abruptly and they launch into a very different version of the march-like second subject (d), now as though on parade as it has never been before.

Expansive arpeggios re-establish the predominance of the soloist, leading to a passage that everyone who knows the concerto awaits with some eagerness. It is an extension of the first theme (a), with a stirring accompaniment in chromatically descending triplets. The music is irresistibly march-like here, and one can almost see banners waving in the breeze, and plumed helmets tossing. After a while the soloist is so carried away that the right hand is thrown completely off the beat as the left hand part bubbles upwards like champagne from the neck of a bottle. Two long-drawn arpeggios in unison touch on B flat major and (immediately) B flat minor before the pianist can refer affectionately to the little woodwind tune (e), this time in C flat major. Soon the woodwind assert a more conventional key by echoing the same motif in B flat major, at which point even the listener who may not be able to identify the more arcane processes of modulation will have a sense of order being restored, of a return to a more familiar world.

It is at this moment that the soloist embarks on the ascending scale in broken octaves that has already been strangely anticipated in the First Concerto (see Example 1b on p. 4). The tension is then cleverly built up until the full orchestra begins what is in effect a rather truncated recapitulation. Unusually it begins in the dominant (B flat), only to start to deviate from exact repetition after a mere four bars, or so it seems. What Beethoven actually does is to by-pass no less than fifty-one bars of the original exposition. To reproduce exactly the initial proportions of this section Beethoven seems to feel would labour the point unnecessarily, and furthermore would take the focus too much away from the soloist. Enough, then, to recall all the most important themes once more, not to mention giving the hardworking pianist a rest!

Once more we hear the summons from the woodwind that alerts

the soloist that it is time to rejoin the fray, and as unobtrusively as before, he or she has a unison chromatic scale leading to a two-bar trill on a high G.

Now Beethoven is particularly ingenious in the construction of this movement. The passage we have just heard, together with that clearly recognisable pianist's entry, gives every indication of being a recapitulation of the traditional type. We are entirely justified in sitting back, taking no more effort to concentrate and assuming that there will be no developments of significance in the rest of the movement. It is a completely wrong assumption. Beethoven has conceived this movement on the grandest possible scale; this 'recapitulation' is false. The true recapitulation lies some eighty-four bars ahead, during which there are a number of interesting new developments. On the other hand, when that original opening reappears, complete with even more elaborate flourishes for the soloist, the subsequent *tutti* is reduced to a minimum. In effect Beethoven has transplanted the bulk of an orchestral reprise so that it now comes substantially earlier than the reappearance of those opening mini-cadenzas. Thus, at the very moment when we least expect it, he can embark in a new direction, which he now proceeds to do.

The high G trill soon reveals itself to be the dominant of C minor, and after a few leisurely arpeggios, the pianist settles down to accompany a somewhat mournful version of the main theme (a), which is taken over in turn by the clarinet, bassoon and flute. For some time the woodwind predominate, but the strings grow increasingly impatient at their enforced idleness. Gradually they make their presence felt with the little rhythmic figure that was a notable feature of the first theme,

until suddenly we arrive at a moment for which there was no precedent in past musical history. For the first time the piano as an instrument takes on the full weight of the woodwind choir, reinforced by horns, trumpets and timpani. Dramatically they propose a C flat harmony, which the pianist hurls back, not in the least overawed by their combined might. Again they attempt to browbeat, again he returns their sally. It is a passage that signals a sort of heroic contest in which a lone figure defies the multitude.

However, to have piano and orchestra alternating is one thing, to have them sounding together is another. Having silenced the opposition, the pianist sets out on a series of scale-like octave passages, which march on steadily (in both hands) while the strings are given comparable scales in contrary motion. It is here that Beethoven seems to have had a slight loss of nerve. The piano's octaves are clearly intended to be played with maximum force, although ultimately there is a hugely drawn-out diminuendo. Now the strings are obviously involved here not in a simple dialogue with the piano but in a virtual trial of strength, for their scales are so planned that they are literally in opposition, descending when the pianist's ascend and vice versa. Unable to hear the effect for himself, Beethoven plays safe and directs the strings to play quietly from the first, only accenting one note at the peak of each phrase. Even that is marked *fp*, which indicates a controlled forte, instantly suppressed. With the power of a modern grand piano it is no longer necessary to rig this contest in the pianist's favour, and I am sure that Beethoven would actually be delighted if we changed his instructions so as to allow the strings to play loudly, thus giving the soloist some resistance.

During this clash of wills the bassoon constantly reminds us of the important fragmentary rhythm taken from the first main theme.

At last, after a long final ascent, the piano's octaves give way to a tender version of the lyrical theme (g), first allotted to the violins. The woodwind seem so enamoured of this that they are not content to leave it solely to the pianist; twice they share it, undisturbed by the restless violas and cellos who, eager to get back to the true recapitulation, fidget excitedly in the background with yet another fragment of the initial theme (a). Growing ever quieter, the piano part seems to climb heavenwards until it is literally out of earshot. The rhythm initiated by the violas grows ever more persistent as it is taken over by an increasing number of instruments; and then, unmistakably this time, the true recapitulation appears, complete with even more showy cascades of notes from the pianist. (Interestingly both here and at the very beginning of the work the loud orchestral E flat chord lacks the usual fifth, B flat, giving the harmony an individual sound that is unique to Beethoven, just as the first chord of the Fourth Concerto is special to him. It is as though he had found a way of appropriating these basic chords and making them his own, so that thereafter nobody could space them in that particular way without instantly evoking memories of one or other of the two works.)

Eight bars of orchestral music are enough to remind us of the original exposition, but then the pianist begins to muse thoughtfully on the theme, taking it ever higher and modulating towards the sub-dominant key of A flat. A solo from the second horn player tells us that it is really the dominant of D flat major and not A flat at all. The piano part once again chatters beguilingly as the horn exchanges phrases with the woodwind; then, with a sudden torrent of notes, Beethoven shifts to C sharp minor, a tonality not previously explored in this movement. In a curiously bell-like passage the second subject reappears; indeed from here on the recapitulation proceeds on a fairly conventional course providing a satisfactory symmetry to the movement. The biggest surprise remaining is the absence of a cadenza; we are justified in expecting one as the orchestra goes through the gestures that would normally precede one, but then Beethoven gives specific instructions to the intending performers. Using the musical *lingua franca* Italian instead of the native German which he increasingly preferred, he wrote on the copy 'Non si fa una Cadenza, ma s'attacca subito il seguente' (Don't make a cadenza, but attack immediately the following.)

Starting with allusions to the all-pervasive military rhythm the passage soon accelerates until a lengthy trill leads to an unadorned statement of the second subject (d) in its original key of E flat minor. Just as before, the horns restore the tune to the major while the pianist adds rippling arpeggios which overlap to delightful effect between the two hands. The minor-major alternation is duplicated by the cellos and basses, but using a somewhat drawn-out version of the 'military' rhythm as a basis, and then, rather surprisingly, the full orchestra quotes yet again the opening notes of the main theme, suggesting that it is going to continue as before.

The pianist will have none of this and interrupts the flow with a striking new figure which we have not heard so far. This becomes a dialogue between piano and orchestra whose music seems to sway to and fro before yielding to the woodwind, who are given a gloriously triumphant version of a tune that originally appeared towards the end of the opening exposition. As before, this resolves into the lyrical tune (g) until repeated chords on the woodwind provide a background for the by now familiar ascending chromatic run on the piano. Coming near the beginning, near the middle, and now nearly at the end of the movement it is a feature that instantly impresses itself on our memories, even though Beethoven finds ways of making it slightly different each time.

A pianistic shimmer (which Rachmaninoff may have subconsciously echoed in the closing bars of the first movement of his Third Concerto) starts a slow descent before a final confirmation of E flat major brings us to the end of this majestic movement. It is on a far larger scale than any of the previous keyboard concertos — fifty-two pages of full score compared to thirty-seven in the Fourth Concerto; but what is most significant is that it changed for ever the relationship between the solo piano and the orchestra. Here we see the emergence of the soloist as hero figure; but in the second movement we see, even more remarkably, the soloist as romantic dreamer.

At the start of the slow movement, Beethoven uses a somewhat similar musical link to the ones that he employed in the Third Concerto; by putting the music in B major he would appear to have chosen a key far removed in the tonal sphere from the E flat major that has so predominated earlier. But on the piano the note E flat can also be regarded as D sharp, and D sharp is the major third of B major — in fact it is the note that tells us whether the chord based on B *is* major or minor. Consequently, although the first chord of this wonderful adagio is a considerable shock to the eye, it is perfectly acceptable to the ear; even though there is a scientific and academic difference between E flat and D sharp (which string players claim to be able to convey), to the average listener the notes are the same. (This is not the place for a dissertation on acoustic theory, but if one plays the chords of C minor, B major and A flat major on a well-tuned piano putting the E flat/D sharp on top, the note will appear to sound subtly different. It may seem something of an auditory illusion but the difference is real nevertheless; owing to the shower of harmonics which cumulatively 'colour' the note, it effectively changes, despite its being the same actual black note on the keyboard.)

For fifteen bars the strings, only occasionally reinforced by the wind, present us with a chorale-like tune of great solemnity that would surely by now have been appropriated by the editors of hymn books, were it not for the fact that the vocal range is perhaps a little much for the average congregation:

Ex. 5b

The pianist ignores this entirely; instead, we find a long descending scale-like passage over a restrained left hand accompaniment. Marked *pp espressivo*, it is extraordinarily effective; although the triplets in the bass seem to be severely classical, the soloist appears to be improvising in an almost trance-like condition. It is this and similar passages that give the movement its romantic flavour, and it is hardly surprising that Schumann, writing his mammoth *Fantasy* (Op. 17) to raise funds for a Beethoven memorial, should have quoted this by implication in his finale. In due course the piano part becomes more openly lyrical as the descending scales flower into a sequential melody. The orchestra remains aloof, gravely modulating into D major to make way for another improvisatory passage matching the first.

The instruction *forte* only occurs twice in the whole movement, once just before the pianist's first entry, and now when there is a sudden thickening of the pianistic texture, with both hands duplicating each other's thirds or sixths in a striking passage which seems to dissolve into a mist of trills; they climb upwards like a somewhat laggardly skylark, only to sink down again to reach the pianist's ultimate acceptance of the original theme. This is presented in a slightly embroidered form before yielding graciously to the woodwind who are entrusted with the tune, with gentle off-beat pizzicato chords for the strings. Meanwhile the piano part consists of a quiet bell-like figure which gradually descends until there is nothing left but an octave B sustained by two bassoons. This, with a couple of confirmatory chords, could easily be the end of the movement, but there would be a nasty jar had Beethoven plunged the music straight into E flat for the final rondo. In fact he devises a positively magical moment in which he exploits exactly the same type of harmonic twist that he had used to bridge the first and second movements. There the tonic note (E flat) was temporarily regarded as D sharp in order to effect a transition to B major; here he slides the B almost imperceptibly to a mysterious B flat on two horns, thus making it become the dominant of E flat. As though still in a dream, the pianist suggests a possible shape for a rondo-theme. Not convinced of its suitability at first, it is tried out again, this time taking it a little further. (It was to serve as a model for Schumann when, in his piano concerto, he was faced with the same problem of linking two movements of very differing moods.)

Then, with an abrupt change from *pp* to *ff*, Beethoven launches into the final rondo with a boisterous theme that is initially based entirely on the notes of the common chord:

Ex. 5c

There is another intriguing link with Schumann here since in his *Carnaval* he quotes a portion of this tune in 'The March of the

Davidites against the Philistines'. (It comes in bars 11–12, and establishes a rhythmic figure that is to prove of great importance later in the movement.)

The orchestra seems almost to reel, such is the impact of this rumbustious melody; then they take it up enthusiastically, under-lining that important rhythm by allowing it to appear on trumpets and horns alone at one point. Not to be outdone, the pianist embarks on a ferocious scale-passage which gradually subsides and gives way to a tune which is to be exclusively reserved for the piano. It has a Schubertian lilt to it, but shows a curious eagerness in its second half, seeming to aspire to ever greater heights with a series of little springing figures:

Ex. 5d

A chirpy bassoon suggests that this really is not the proper thing in a serious concerto and proffers a simple descending scale of B flat. This proves to be not a bad idea, and it is tried out several times by soloist and orchestra in turn in a playful exchange which alternates between tentative and forceful. Soon a new tune appears over a busily accompanying left hand; again it is exclusive to the soloist, who at one point is so carried away as to break momentarily into a clear four-in-bar, a cross accentuation that explodes into some feverish broken octaves before returning to the main theme.

This, the third appearance of the tune, soon gives way to a deli-cious mock fugue in which the strings assume a professorial man-ner in their treatment of bars 11–12 of the theme while the piano part seems literally to run rings around them. The mood is not at all

Beethoven's mature concertos is the masterly way with which he
catches our attention with the very opening bars; the unostenta-
tious beginning of the Fourth Concerto, the flamboyant gestures at
the start of the Fifth Concerto and the unaccompanied cellos and
basses which begin the Triple Concerto, all these were totally
unexpected, calculated to take an audience unawares. The four
quiet beats on the drum which open this work are equally unpredictable, and provide further evidence of Beethoven's imaginative
liberation of the timpani from their hitherto conventional role.[1]
Even the subsequent chorale-like tune is a surprise in that it is
scored for woodwind alone when we traditionally might expect
strings:

Ex. VCa

When the orchestral violins do appear it is on a note that seems to
violate all that has gone before. With an air of tranquillity the
woodwind have established D major as the tonic key; the D *sharp*
that the violins now suggest (in an echo of the first-bar rhythm)
must have seemed an outrage to a contemporary audience and
even now preserves something of its surprise effect. D major is
restored quite forcibly in the very next bar, as though Beethoven
(or perhaps the strings themselves) were apologising for so blatant
an indiscretion. The second violins and violas now proffer the
four-times repeated D sharp again as though querying Beethoven's
intentions. Equally emphatically Beethoven restores propriety
with a return to D major, unpolluted by this alien accidental. Its
presence will ultimately be explained when we come to the closing bars of the second subject, but at this stage we are meant to be
puzzled. The restoration of D major is confirmed by some
leisurely rising scale-passage in the woodwind.

Suddenly the calm is shattered by a violent switch into B flat major, a move so unexpected that Beethoven gives us a moment's silence to let it sink in. The agitation prevails for several bars and we are justified in expecting a substantial development in this mood; instead it dwindles into some brief phrases for the first violins which lead to the true second subject. This too is given to the woodwind, its essentially lyrical phrases being accompanied by the opening drum-rhythm, now given to the first violins:

Ex. VCb

Its transference into the minor by the strings gives it a somewhat forlorn air, but emotions are kept in check by the severe repetition of the by-now familiar quadruple beat derived from bar I; solemnly reiterated by trumpets, horns and timpani it effectively establishes a relationship between first and second subjects. Meanwhile the violas and cellos have a busy triplet figure which tends to go in contrary motion to the melody, falling when it rises and vice versa. Briefly the woodwind reinforce the violins before the enigma of that 'alien' D sharp is finally explained as the tune is turned in a new direction to touching effect:

Ex. VCc

It may be a fanciful interpretation but Beethoven appears so delighted to show that he knew from the first that the mysterious D sharp was a tease, a note that could ultimately be integrated as it is here; triumphantly, point made, he restores the music to the 'proper' key of D major. At this point he introduces us to a new and proud theme which is instantly seized upon enthusiastically by the cellos and basses:

Ex. VCd

V'cellos
(an octave lower)

Just at the moment when the music seems to be heading for a final cadence in D we are left in suspense as the phrase checks in mid-flight on the dominant, quietens with a descending sigh and, as it were, bows politely to usher in the soloist.

An interesting inversion follows, for the last orchestral notes are G,E,C♯,A which are now reversed by the soloist into A,C♯,E,G. With a flight of broken octaves extending upwards to a top G, the soloist embarks on a brief cadenza which covers a range of some three and a half octaves culminating in an ascent to a high D. As it progresses it should be noted that there is a subtle allusion to the second subject; this part of the phrase –

is transformed into

Whether this was dictated by Beethoven's subconscious or whether it was an act of craftsmanship we shall never know, but the correlation between the two passages is intriguing.

The orchestra is now given an almost exact repetition of the first twenty-four bars, above which the soloist adds elegant decorations until the ascending scales in the woodwind. These are deftly turned into the minor with the next entry which takes us progres-

77

sively through F major and A minor in a display of agility markedly different from anything that we have heard so far.

At last the second subject reappears, now in the dominant key of A; as before, this is changed to the minor by the orchestra while the soloist provides a much elaborated version of the triplets which were originally given to the lower strings. Allowing for the necessary transpositions the parallels with the original exposition are almost exact. Only with an extension of the theme shown in Ex. VCd does Beethoven begin to break new ground. As he does so the violin part becomes increasingly busy until the orchestra players are reduced to the role of admiring spectators.

We have now arrived at one of the most magical moments in the whole concerto; after several ventures into its upper range, the violin part settles on a quiet and sustained trill; softly the violins remind us once more of the four repeated notes, this time on E, the dominant of A major which itself is the dominant of the 'home' key. They are answered by a ghostly F natural far below; again they repeat the fourfold E, ascending this time to the mysterious F. Venturing into the unfamiliar tonality of C major (contradicting the very notes which best identify the home key of D) rising chords, together with an ascending trill from the soloist, lead us safely back to A major. A series of scale-like passages on the violin seem about to confirm this when suddenly there is a violent interruption from the whole orchestra. It is a passage which caught us by surprise once before, but this time it has the effect of reassuring us that we are 'back on course' again. This is reinforced by a substantial recapitulation although for the most part it is more forcibly expressed. Only the tonalities are different, with A minor and C major predominating; otherwise all is as it was before, including even an exact transposition of the opening cadenza. It is a moment for Beethoven to show his creative genius. Instead of extending this recapitulation much further, thereby becoming utterly predictable, he begins a wonderful development of the very opening theme, a theme which has been curiously neglected up to now. A shift of a semitone (F natural to F sharp) takes us into the so-far unvisited realms of B minor, whereupon, having reminded us poignantly of the theme, the violinist begins a rambling sequence of triplets whose purpose is essentially to accompany a pair of serious, and nor surely is the outburst of apparent rage which the pianist is shortly given. Forgiveness comes with the happy fourth version of the rondo-theme which now ensues in the unfamiliar key of C major. Beethoven continues in this new tonality for some time with music that chatters away to no great consequence but quite loudly – it is marked *sempre forte* (always loud) in the score.

Two horns quietly emphasise that important rhythm, restoring E flat to our ears as a possible return to 'home' as they do so. 'Not a bit of it', says Beethoven, and starts a deliciously frivolous fifth version, now in the sub-dominant key of A flat. However, he soon thinks better of it and wanders happily through a series of chromatic runs in the extreme upper register of the keyboard.

After a little repetition of past events, suitably transposed of course, he catches us unawares with a sudden transition into the totally unexpected key of E major, a tonality that contradicts every single note of the E flat scale which constitutes the 'proper' key. Bassoon and oboe (that rhythm again) provide the means of access to this alien territory; the pianist seems slightly incredulous, and not unnaturally begins this, the seventh version, *pp*. The ensuing passage confirms that this is really the key Beethoven intends and the music grows in confidence, with cascades of scales, rising in the left hand, falling in the right.

The pianist begins the tortuous journey back to E flat with a long modulatory passage which is rather suggestive of an angry cellist practising across the strings. The orchestra seem obsessed with that pervasive rhythm, passing it from violas to violins in turn, and then more forcefully to the wind. A quiet trill tells us that a route back to the home key of E flat has been found at last, and the strings gently remind us of the pianist's first tentative glimpse of the rondo-theme that had originally provided such a magical link between the two movements.

Triumphantly the pianist restates the main tune in its entirety and a full scale recapitulation begins. This follows a conventional and predictable course until we encounter a brief diversion into A flat and yet another version of the theme, this time divided between soloist and orchestra.

Like a swarm of angered hornets the orchestra return to the tonic (E flat) and loudly proclaim the theme in fast repeated notes that are in danger of inviting Sir Henry Wood's immortal rebuke to the violins – 'There you are, sawing away regardless!' The pianist responds in happy-go-lucky mood, setting many a foot tapping in the audience, so lilting is the rhythm. Once more bars 11–12 prove invaluable, providing the orchestra with relevant material while the soloist joyfully shows off with thunderous arpeggios.

In a remarkable coda, the timpani player constantly reminds us of the motto rhythm as the piano part starts a slow descent through a series of beautifully spaced chords. Finally the music appears to have come to a complete halt, as though Beethoven's inspiration has truly failed him. Just when it seems that total exhaustion has set in, the pianist, in a sudden burst of renewed energy, embarks on a virtuoso scale-passage that, ultimately aided by the full orchestra, brings this masterpiece to a glorious conclusion.

Were the citizens of Vienna so imperceptive that they did not realise that this magnificent work was to be a landmark in musical history? It seems so; but in later years restitution has been made, for no aspiring concert pianist can afford to neglect it, nor will audiences of today fail to appreciate its stature. Here indeed the pianist's hands bestride the keyboard like a colossus, establishing a towering mastery over the orchestra that brooks no resistance.

Notes

1. The four exclamation marks show the intensity of his feelings, which he appears to have preferred to vent on paper rather than person-to-person. This was not uncommon with Beethoven; the famous Heilingenstadt Testament in which he lays bare his most intimate fears of deafness to his brother Karl was, it seems, not actually sent, nor were the so-called letters to the 'Immortal Beloved'. Neurotics of the present-day confess their innermost feelings to a psychiatrist; Beethoven relied on mere paper.
2. Extract from *Thayer's Life of Beethoven*, orig. trans. by H.E. Krehbiel, revised by E. Forbes, Princeton, 1964.
3. The collapse of tonality initiated by later composers such as Liszt and Wagner was still to come; for the time being everyone, audiences included, valued the anchor of key.

Violin Concerto in
D Major, Op. 61

1 Flute; 2 Oboes; 2 Clarinets; 2 Bassoons; 2 Horns; 2 Trumpets; 2 Timpani; Strings.

Nowadays, the first performance of a violin concerto by a major composer would be treated as an important event in the musical calendar; critics would no doubt be invited to rehearsals to get a preliminary hearing of the work, and might even be loaned photocopies of the score; profiles of the composer listing past achievements would appear in the Sunday papers; Radio 3 would provide an introductory discussion before broadcasting the concert live and even enable those of us who had missed it to hear a recorded repeat a few days later. If the concerto failed to be adopted into the repertoire we could feel sympathy for the composer and for the soloist; if it succeeded, we could hail it as a rare triumph and add the inevitable CD to our Christmas shopping list.

How unfortunate by comparison was Beethoven; his stature as a major composer was undoubtedly acknowledged in Vienna, but even so the violin concerto was treated shamefully at its première. In the first place it was divided into two halves, the first movement to be played before the interval, the remainder after a substantial break. This could perhaps have given the soloist a chance to take a look at the finale since both he and the orchestra were actually sightreading the piece, having had no rehearsal. Instead, he chose to fill the time by entertaining the audience with a violin solo of his own composition, to be played on one string only with the instrument held upside down. Beethoven's concerto was clearly of secondary importance, as a contemporary account seems to suggest:

> Among other excellent pieces the remarkable violinist Clement also played a violin concerto by Beethoven which, owing to its originalities and wealth of beautiful passages, was received with exceptionally great applause.... The opinion of connoisseurs ... admits that it contains beautiful passages but confesses that the context often seems broken and that the endless repetition of unimportant passages produces a tiring effect.

With such an unpropitious launch it is not entirely surprising that publication was long delayed. Despite the 'exceptionally great applause' (probably more for the soloist than the work itself), several publishing houses turned it down and no full score was printed until 1894, 88 years after the first performance. Only when the twelve-year old prodigy Joachim played it with the ever-enterprising Mendelssohn conducting did the concert-going public really take it to their hearts. Even with our delight in sensationalism it is doubtful if any manager of today would allow a twelve-year old to make a mark with this particular work; it is too much to expect a child to plumb its spiritual depths, and a display of gymnastic prowess would seem more impressive in something rather more superficial. Not unlike the Fourth Piano Concerto (Op. 58), the Violin Concerto makes its points without any undue emphasis, sharing with that work an undeniable technical difficulty that yet avoids virtuosity for virtuosity's sake.

No doubt disappointed by the lack of interest shown by publishers at the time, Beethoven soon prepared an alternative version for solo piano and orchestra; it was done at the request of Muzio Clementi who, in addition to being a brilliant pianist and composer, was a successful publisher and wanted to present the piano version in an English edition. It seems ironic that in this form, specifically designed to make it more popular, the work has never caught on, whereas there are now over thirty editions of it as originally intended for violin.

One of the outstanding features to be appreciated in

major, E major, and to D, therefore a continuation in G gives a feeling of stability to the movement, not in the least wearisome.

Only by the most devious methods can this new development be described as another variation, yet it is not long before the solo part returns at least to the second half of the theme before wandering free again, with hushed strings and quiet horns in attendance. This whole section is best regarded as an interlude designed to break away from the rigid framework of strict variation form. Yet the movement is so imaginatively contrived that it seems Beethoven is bound by his love for the theme and its mood, rather than by the requirements of academic correctness.

The horns again act as a quiet, restraining influence, preventing the soloist from straying too far from the matter in hand; then they softly remind us of the opening notes of the movement, leading us to expect a reprise of the long neglected theme. With a sudden awakening, Beethoven shatters the dream-like spell of these closing bars, leaving the violinist to execute a powerful trill and a brief link into the finale.

There is a rustic quality to the theme of this Rondo, not unlike the country music-making that Beethoven immortalised in the 'Pastoral' Symphony. The rudimentary accompaniment provided by the cellos subtly suggests the soft rhythmic clapping of hands as though a few listeners might be sitting in the parlour of a village inn; one feels that Beethoven is in what he called his 'unbuttoned' mood, more at ease with his surroundings in a snuggery than he would ever be in a concert-hall.

Ex. VCf

The concluding phrase is briefly echoed by oboes and horns before the theme is repeated two octaves higher, this time with a tentative accompaniment by the violins.

Up to this point the presentation of the theme has been intimate with orchestral support at its minimal; then, suddenly, like guests hitherto concealed at a surprise birthday party, the whole orchestra bursts in fortissimo in a raucous *tutti* which adds a further extension to the theme in the shape of a decorated descending scale. It makes the feeling of a rustic dance even more evident, and one can easily imagine gnarled hands slapping bare thighs in the traditional Austrian manner.

Naively descriptive music was much in vogue at this time and as the *Pastoral Symphony*, or the *Les Adieux* sonata indicate Beethoven was not entirely averse to employing it. Here the sound of horns suggests that hunters are not far away. The violinist seems inspired by the phrase, tosses it into a higher register, and uses it too as a basis for some increasingly athletic passages. The persistent hunting-horn motif may conjure up an image of horses and riders in our minds but the virtuosity demanded by the violin part soon brings us back to more purely musical matters.

For a time the violinist is wholly preoccupied with dazzingly brilliant semiquavers, disregarding the tentative suggestions of the rondo-theme which come with increasing emphasis from the string section. The addition of oboes and bassoons to the texture finally brings the episode to an end, and after a slight pause the original theme is resumed exactly as it was.

This time the loud ensuing outburst from the orchestra takes a new direction after a mere four bars; introducing F naturals for the first time, the music passes swiftly through D minor, E flat major, F major and then back to D major again. But is it? Once again we need to become aware of the subtlety of the musical language; although the *notes* seem to be in D major their *function* is no longer that of a 'tonic', a 'home' key; instead they have become the dominant of G minor.

The soloist appears to think about the full implications of this for some three unaccompanied bars before introducing an entirely new theme in that key:

Ex. VCg

etc.

I was once taken to task by a critic for attaching frivolous words to this tune, taking its limerick-like rhythm as inspiration. (It was about 'A certain young lady of Bonn', but no matter!) We often treat a work of this quality with an inappropriate degree of reverence. Beethoven's sense of humour is well documented and I have sometimes described him as the sort of person who delights in asking you to sit down, only to whip the chair from under you just as you are about to do so; instances of equivalent practical jokes in his music abound. If he really had intended us to take this tune seriously he surely would not have given it later to a solo bassoon with the sort of 'pom-ching-ching' accompaniment that even a pub pianist could easily vamp. It is Beethoven who dictates the content of a passage not us; we may interpret it wrongly, but it is at least worthwhile to look at the music with an unprejudiced eye – I say 'look', because in performance the essential humour of episodes such as these is seldom conveyed.

The end of the vamping accompaniment signals a return to a more serious approach as the soloist adopts a more graceful and decorative style in the second half of the tune, but Beethoven cannot resist returning to the bassoon with its happy if slightly silly dance-tune. A pair of oboes take up the refrain, but once more it is the strings, this time in unison, who remind us of the real theme of the movement, calling us back from this jolly diversion with a quite stern reappraisal of its opening notes.

After a bold display of broken octaves, the violinist takes the hint and restates the rondo-theme exactly as it was. This time the ensuing orchestral outburst could be described as a true recapitulation since bar for bar it is a duplicate of what went before, complete with the decorated downward scale extension of the tune.

Impatiently the soloist snatches the last bar of this reprise away from the orchestra with four amusing pizzicato notes, and then it seems the hunt returns as again we hear the horns and their distinctive call. After much activity based on this idea we can hear a number of quiet reminders of the proper subject, sometimes in the strings, sometimes in the woodwind; the violin part chatters away unceasingly, seemingly heedless despite the occasionally quite powerful emphasis on the opening few notes that comes from the basses. Impressively the hunting horn theme returns on horns and oboes and then the full orchestra, coming to a majestic halt as prelude to a cadenza.

Once more, perhaps not anticipating what horrors might be committed in his name, Beethoven leaves its composition entirely to the soloist who is at liberty to go musically where his fancy leads him. (Judging from Clement's earlier displays in the middle of the concert, farmyard imitations or birdsong might have been on offer!) However, as is often the case, Beethoven's way of emerging from the cadenza is brilliantly original. Far beneath the ultimate trill (which is conventionally expected) the cellos and basses offer a confident reference to the main theme. Receiving neither acknowledgement nor recognition from the soloist trilling happily above, they gradually lose all confidence before wandering questioningly into the alien tonality of A flat major:

Ex. VCh

The violins take a little convincing and seem to doubt the wisdom of the move, but the soloist endorses it with a delightful restatement of the theme in the new key. For a time the music is marked *sempre pp*, a reminder from the composer that the magical fairy-like mood should be maintained despite the increasingly elaborate writing for the solo part. A series of gentle modulatory chords leads the music back to D major, a destination which is serenely confirmed by four leisurely and unaccompanied notes from the soloist.

We have reached the coda which is traditionally taken at a slightly easier tempo to start with. Harmoniously the woodwind toy with those opening five notes, the soloist intervening with a new answering phrase. This enchanting duet is the cue for the first violins to join the game, until everyone catches the increasingly boisterous mood, ultimately throwing the rhythms off the beat in sheer exuberance. All seems as if it is going to end quite rowdily but Beethoven has one more surprise for us; suddenly the music grows quieter, lingering on the notes of D major as if uncertain of quite what to do. Then, in a moment of supremely imaginative composition, Beethoven presents us with a last glimpse of the rondo theme on the violin alone. While this is marked *pp*, soloists sometimes arrogantly disregard Beethoven's instruction, unable to resist the opportunity to impress the audience one last time, but it should be played in such a way as to make the final two whacking great chords a real surprise. They are the culmination of one of the greatest, some people maintain *the* greatest violin concerto ever written; violinists will forever continue to study it, seeking to penetrate its depths and uncover its secrets. We in the audience must never let familiarity lead us to take it for granted for without it music would indeed be the poorer.

Notes

1. Beethoven was perhaps the first composer to free the timpani from their hitherto hum-drum role; think of the timpanist's unique duet with the piano near the end of the *Emperor*, or the electrifying interpolations of the timpani in the scherzo of The Ninth Symphony.

2. Although he had learned the violin as a child Beethoven was by no means the accomplished player that (for instance) Mozart was. It could therefore have been prudence as much as custom that led him merely to leave a space for a cadenza, although one shudders to think what Clement may have provided at that first performance. There now exist more than thirty different cadenzas from various hands, but the one most frequently played and usually regarded as the most satisfactory is Joachim's; however all of them must end as Beethoven intended.

Triple Concerto,
Op. 56

1 Flute; 2 Oboes; 2 Clarinets; 2 Bassoons; 2 Horns; 2 Trumpets; Timpani; Strings.

Opportunities to hear the Triple Concerto, particularly in performance, do not occur all that often; one can scour the programmes of the world's finest orchestras without coming across it. It seems to appear only in comprehensive Beethoven festivals, and then perhaps because the organisers feel it *ought* to be done rather than because of a compulsion to do it. Yet the opus number tells us that this work was written in Beethoven's prime; 1804–5 was one of his most fruitful periods, coming between the Third and Fourth Symphonies and coinciding with the three piano sonatas, Op. 53, 54 and 57 as well as the so-called Rasumovsky quartets; moreover he was already working on the first version of *Fidelio*. Does it, then, represent a lapse on Beethoven's part, a lowering of his high standards, or is its relative neglect due to other causes?

Partly, of course, the reason must be financial. To engage three artists whose names are sufficiently well-known to appeal to the public will obviously cost three times as much as employing any one of them; furthermore it is unlikely that the players will have studied the work independently and therefore each will have to learn the actual notes especially for the occasion; rehearsals will have to be fitted into busy schedules, for it is unthinkable that the three soloists should meet for the first time at an orchestral rehearsal. The solution that is usually adopted is to engage a trio accustomed to playing together, despite public scepticism that this has financial rather than artistic motivations.

If we think for a moment about the format of the Triple Concerto we can see that there is one major musical problem intrinsic to it; if the performers are to be treated in such a way that they are to be regarded as equal in the distribution of material, it follows that any theme of significance must be played three times over before any development can be contemplated. This has the effect of holding back the natural progress of the music; impatient as we are to 'get on with it' we are able to predict too clearly the third presentation of any idea of importance; moreover, partly as a consequence of this, there is rather too much of C major to be found, especially in the last movement. This would have been acceptable in Beethoven's day but we have experienced the harmonic developments of nearly two centuries and are considerably more sophisticated in our tastes.

As was only too often the case at the first performance of Beethoven's works preparation seems to have been inadequate. Beethoven's biographer Anton Schindler, who was present, tells us that the artists did not take 'sufficient care' and that there was 'no applause'.[1] It was not until twenty-two years later, in 1830, that a second performance was forthcoming; this time it was enthusiastically received so one assumes that the soloists had been rather more conscientious. It is interesting that Beethoven appears to have had a performance in mind in 1807, for in a letter he wrote in that year he refers to it as a *'concertante'* and mentions two players, Seidler the violinist and a noted cellist called Kraft.[2] He requests the urgent return of the piano part from a Herr Bigot (Count Rasumovsky's librarian) as he had been reproached by his publishers for not sending it, and while there is no word about an actual performance it is surely more than a coincidence that these two names are quoted in the same letter; both were in the service of the Archduke Rudolph for whom the piano part was certainly written. The Archduke was a favourite pupil of Beethoven's for whose somewhat limited technique due allowance was made. Of course it is always possible that he was involved in a private performance in his palace but no record of such an occasion exists. The apparent need for urgency was misplaced as no performance materialised as far as is known until after Beethoven's death.

The work begins in an unusual fashion with the cellos and basses in quiet unison:

Ex. TCa

The dominant, G, is confirmed by three repetitions, although at this stage all is hushed save for a single intrusive chord from the horns. The strings now begin a crescendo in which a slightly modified version of the opening bar is built progressively through the basic notes of the C major chord until, by the time the twenty-first bar of the movement is reached, the entire orchestra is involved. Notice especially the very active part for the cellos and basses, harbingers no doubt of the sort of writing Beethoven had in mind for the solo cellist at a later stage. After several strident bars which culminate in a grand orchestral unison, the first violins begin a theme which derives its rhythm from the opening phrase but which is otherwise new:

Ex. TCb

Whether it is the true second subject we are not to know at the time as another possible candidate for that honour is due to appear a few moments later; certainly we should store it in our memories as something that is sure to appear again. Suddenly its forward impulse is arrested as the strings come to rest on an F major chord. Mysteriously it changes to the minor, leading to a brief but memorably beautiful excursion into A flat major which sadly never occurs again.

Bustling triplets from the second violins lead to a new theme which uses the rhythm from bar 4 as its springboard:

Ex. TCc

Beethoven almost certainly had memories of a yodel in mind, and the Viennese audience may well have responded to this touch of local colour. Soon, however, he shows a rather sterner side as the brass enter once more in peremptory fashion. Emphatically the full orchestra proclaims the fundamental chords of the key of G major (the dominant) before a few more leisurely notes lead back to C. The end of the introductory *tutti* is confirmed with several loud chords; the soloists have waited their turn long enough. Who will be the first to make his presence felt, we wonder, as the first violins gently reiterate a C; it is almost like the ticking of a clock as we wait, tension building as expectancy mounts.

It is the cello, surprisingly the real leader throughout, who is given the honour, and his entry reveals a rather fascinating clash. It can be seen from Example TCa that the first brief phrase ends on a D, which is also the starting point of the second phrase; the first violins persist with their 'ticking' while the violas proffer a tentative B in a rhythm which curiously anticipates the drum motif of the violin concerto. That is no more than a coincidence; what is striking is that at this moment Beethoven has three adjacent notes (B,C and D) sounding simultaneously, a mixture that must indeed have seemed daring in the early 1800s and which adds a consider-able touch of spice to the harmony. As the cello part rises phrase by phrase the violas have an opposite downward progression, so that that we feel that the music is gradually opening out as it is in those time-lapse films in which a flower is seen to accomplish a week's growth in a matter of seconds.

A smooth transition to the dominant leads logically to the vio-linist's entry; it soon becomes a neat little dialogue with the cello in which they exchange the snippets in bars 4/5 of the opening theme before joining in a busy passage in triplets which slows expressively to make way for the pianist. Perhaps feeling that his pupil the Archduke might be nervous at his first entry, Beethoven gives him the theme in simple octaves. The cello accompanies him with gruff semiquavers while the violin makes polite comments. Soon these rather deferential passages are replaced by rushing scales; in time the pianist is left by himself to perform a chromatic scale with the hands a third apart, something which Beethoven surely must have made the sixteen-year-old Rudolph do in his lessons. It should never be forgotten that Beethoven had his pupil in mind for the first performance, even though the plan came to naught.

Four bars from the full orchestra confirm that C major is indeed the proper key; in doing so they introduce a new theme which the cellist takes up enthusiastically, accompanied discreetly by the pianist:

Ex. TCd

The violinist, perhaps feeling that his colleagues are having too easy a time, has an elaborate little variation which climbs into the highest register before making a gracious descent into less perilous spheres.

And now, after a brief interlude in which the young Archduke can show that he has practised broken octaves, albeit on the white notes, he is allowed a new theme all on his own. It is such a one as Mozart might well have written, complete with turns and trills that give it an eighteenth century flavour. It is imitated by the cellist, but soon gives way to an exchange of triplets between the three soloists that possibly provided Beethoven with an idea he was later to use in the still-to-be-written Fourth Concerto. (He habitually had several compositions in his mind at one time and their opus numbers are nearly consecutive.)

A strong intervention by the orchestra tells us that we have reached not E major but the dominant of A – the question remains is it A *minor* or A *major*? It comes as something of a surprise to discover that it is the latter, since this involves sharpening the C natural that is the tonal base of the work.

After a cadenza-like passage from the pianist, again based on very Mozartean figuration, the cello and the violin in turn show us that Example TCb was indeed the second subject, its appearance in this new key giving it a delightful freshness. The orchestra is not to be denied a share of this novel tonality but the soloists, led this time by the pianist, soon embark on a particularly lovely modulatory passage that leads us gently from E major through D minor, B flat major to F major. Just as we think that we are about to settle on this as our final destination, we find the music changes direction and ascends once more, this time to a very definite A minor.

A stormy section ensues, with a ferocious rocking figure on the violin and a striking variation on Example TCb on the cello:

Ex. TCe

For a time, the writing for the two string instruments is quite wild, with the orchestra reduced to playing a rhythmic accompaniment in hushed awe. Soon the pianist joins the fray and a quite lengthy passage follows in which all three soloists are busily engaged in a torrent of semiquavers. It is one of the most brilliant episodes in the whole work and ends with the pianist triumphant. Suddenly, and quite unexpectedly, the cellist calms everything down with a restraining phrase, acknowledged in turn by piano and violin, before rushing scales usher in a powerful orchestral *tutti*. All of the ascending scales which precede it lead us to expect that this will be in A minor, the key to which they seem to be inevitably heading. Skilfully Beethoven avoids the obvious and sidesteps into F major, and then, realising that a goal so thoroughly prepared cannot be avoided, settles for A minor after all, confirming that this time he is in earnest, with a series of thumping cadences. Meanwhile the soloists no doubt welcome the opportunity to mop their brows!

There follows a recapitulation (or so we suppose) in a very unorthodox A major. Our suspicions should surely be aroused by the unusual key yet all seems normal otherwise. As before it is the cello who begins, after a somewhat misleading preliminary passage which suggests we are on the brink of new developments. For the time being the new tonality is novelty enough, added to the fact that the cello part now lies a sixth higher. The violins resume their 'ticking' repetition on the new key note, we still find those remarkable clashes, now G sharp and A against B, and everything proceeds in textbook fashion until the pianist has reached his fourth phrase. Twenty-five bars of the original exposition of the soloists have been exactly duplicated before Beethoven breaks away and embarks on an impassioned exchange of arpeggios between the two string players and the pianist.

In its storm-tossed way this passage is not unlike that which comes in the development of the so-called *Waldstein Sonata* (Op. 53) on which Beethoven may well have been working at the time. Rather forlornly, as though with little hope of it being heard, the woodwind constantly remind the soloists of the first subject by offering the second half of bar 1, or fragments clearly derived from it.

The cellist emerges from this maelstrom with a lyrical theme that strongly resembles a passage from the first movement of the Third Piano Concerto; no conscious allusion could have been intended by Beethoven but it is not surprising if occasionally ideas from the past resurfaced; what is more surprising is that it happened so seldom. It may well be that finding himself in C minor, the key of the concerto, was sufficient to prompt an unconscious reaction; after all, the basic structure of the theme is nothing but a descending scale with an attractive lingering on certain of the notes:

Ex. TCf (cf Ex. 3b)

(cantabile)   etc.

The violinist is attracted to this but the pianist seems to doubt its relevance and time and again reminds us of the very opening rhythm. Since these reminders are in the left hand it is only natural for the cellist to be the first to take the hint. Soon the dialogue is drowned in a tumult of rising scales which ultimately lead to a majestic reprise of the initial theme from the full orchestra. It is the true recapitulation, long-postponed, but now thunderous where it was once reticent.

To start with, the music proceeds in a totally predictable manner with the same build-up as before; this time violin and cello are not kept waiting as long as they were previously, and soon they add decorative, if somewhat spiky, arpeggios to the salient orchestral chords. (Their figuration was no doubt inspired by the *Waldstein*-like episode that came earlier.)

If we understand the normal conventions of a sonata-form movement (which of course also apply to the structure of a concerto, although with the necessary modifications) this is the point at which we might expect Ex. TCb to make a reappearance as the second subject. Instead, the cellist launches into another lyrical tune not unlike Ex. TCf in its initial notes but in fact consisting of the second half of Ex. TCd, now accompanied as before by the piano in a register which, although it sounds gruff today, was doubtless more acceptable on an instrument of Beethoven's time.

In going straight to this theme Beethoven has effected a shrewd cut of some ninety bars, but thereafter he is happy to stick to an almost exact repetition of earlier events apart from a diversion into an unexpected major key at one point. Finally a passage is reached which bears all the signs of being the loud preliminary chords prior to a cadenza. Now both Haydn and Mozart have written cadenzas in which several instruments were involved; one thinks of the *Et incarnatus est* from Mozart's C minor Mass, in which the soprano soloist supplies but one thread in a marvellous web of woodwind counterpoint. But a cadenza for these particular instruments is a problem which it seems Beethoven was not willing to tackle; it could so easily sound like a misplaced extract from a piano trio which so far he has managed mostly to avoid. Instead he reverts to the yodelling theme shown in Ex. TCc, and which he seems to have neglected entirely since it first appeared in the opening *tutti*.

To those of an academic and analytical mind it could be regarded as the beginning of a fairly lengthy coda; at any rate it is the signal for some elaborate runs on scale patterns from all three players as well as some passages which are brief recollections of past events. Then a quickening of tempo is indicated and the movement hastens to its (very conclusive!) ending, the chords of C major and its dominant resounding in our ears.

In the slow movement which follows Beethoven gives us a frustrating vision of what a wonderful concerto for cello he might have written had he put his mind to it. The pianist is reduced to the role of accompanist throughout the movement and is never allowed the songlike theme which is introduced at first by muted strings but taken over by the cellist, who cannot resist joining them:

Ex. TCg

The tune is extended for a further twelve bars by the soloist with a phrase that reaches ever higher before it finally settles gently to rest.[3] If for any reason the Triple Concerto deserves a more frequent airing it is to be found here, for this melody is one of Beethoven's finest inspirations.

The pianist joins in with elaborately decorated passages based on a rising chord of A flat which in time become nothing more than accompanying arpeggios of a purely supportive nature. At no point is he entrusted with anything of thematic importance, and whether the young Archduke resented this or felt rather relieved we shall never know.

The movement is unusually short, being little more than the theme twice through (as though indeed it were two verses of a song) followed by a decorated excursion into G major, on which key Beethoven seems to deliberate for some time before revealing that it must be the dominant, leading inevitably to the C major of the finale. Before this begins there is an amusing passage in which the cellist has no fewer than forty-five increasingly rapid reiterations of the same G before finally plucking up sufficient courage to launch into the last movement.

The instruction 'Rondo all Polacca' simply means that the Rondo is in the rhythm of a Polonaise, for which 'Polacca' is the Italian; however it should be understood that this should not suggest any close relationship to Chopin's conception, even though the characteristic rhythm

does occur quite extensively in the middle of the movement. The tune is in fact extremely bland, and is accompanied by gently paired semiquavers on the violins:

Ex. TCh

The neat twist at the end enables the violinist to repeat the tune in E major, turning it back to the home key every bit as neatly as it ends. Very quietly the woodwind suggest the traditional polonaise rhythm, although curiously for a moment or two the music sounds extraordinarily Mozartean.

With the pianist's entry, marked '*sempre pp*', a new fragmentary figure is introduced:

Ex. TCi

The two string players, as though scorning such childish simplicities, surround them with elaborate arpeggios whose arch-like span covers several octaves at a time. These evolve into scurrying runs which come to an exhausted halt on a huge dominant chord. The orchestra, momentarily outclassed and indeed flabbergasted, confirm that this is a landmark worth noting; there is a pause, as if to allow us to take breath after this brief spell of virtuosity.

Tentatively the pianist proffers some repeated quaver G's, which are echoed almost in disbelief by the two string players in an exchange which sounds remarkably as though Beethoven, always a martyr to digestive problems, was succumbing to an attack of musical hiccups. All three now have the tune in unison; this time its second half is taken over loudly by the entire orchestra, ending without the diversion into E.

A few bars of busy semiquavers in a sturdy unison lead us to the second subject. This is one of the few points where one cannot help feeling that Beethoven has miscalculated by giving us a surfeit of C major: indeed, as much had been hinted earlier in this chapter there is nothing wrong with the subject itself, but the previous bars give every indication of modulating into the dominant, the proper key for a second subject. Instead, Beethoven, rather weakly in my opinion, returns to C and this tune with its coquettish 'Scotch snap':

Ex. TCj

Enjoyable though this is it simply takes us back to a thumping C major, endorsed by all three soloists. Playfully, they introduce a series of running passages which, however, do not break away from the restriction of the tonality. The pianist does try, in a modulatory passage which passes briefly through several keys before arriving a mite predictably on the overdue dominant. In the Second Piano Concerto, first movement, there is a left-hand run which accomplishes a rather similar journey in a considerably more enterprising way. Here, perhaps in deference to the Archduke, the music is a little suggestive of a technical exercise.

The cellist now introduces a new theme to which the violinist adds agreeable little comments:

Ex. TCk

After this has been suitably embellished, there is a suggestion of a cadenza for the three instruments in a welter of scale-like runs which, after seeming to be heading back home to C, actually stay firmly in G.

Orchestra and soloists join forces next in a further exploration of the potential of Ex. TCk; this time the triple cadenza does return to C, although the soloists seem to be not totally convinced. This is evinced by a strange little section where they linger doubtingly on the notes of the C major chord before settling finally on its dominant. At last the dithering is resolved, and with a trill from the cello the original rondo theme at last returns. As before the subtle twist at the end of the tune turns towards E major, a key doubly welcome after such a lengthy spell in C.

Everything proceeds exactly as before – too much so some would say – and it is some forty bars before we find the music taking any significantly new direction. This happens in the midst of a substantial orchestral *tutti* which leads us to the truly polonaise-like section in A minor mentioned above.

The new tune which is now introduced by the violin is essentially little more than a scale:

Ex. TCl

but as can be seen it modulates back to C, in which key it is now given to the cello.

A considerable episode now ensues in which Beethoven, at first vacillating between these two keys, occasionally flirts with other tonalities. In due course the cellist tires of this and discovers a brand-new tune:

Ex. TCm

The violinist is so taken with this that he cannot resist joining in, and the two of them continue merrily for some time with the pianist accompanying in a fairly routine way.

At last, with a thundering rumble in the bass, he seems to suggest that this is altogether too frivolous. Rather seriously he introduces an arpeggio figure in triplets which unexpectedly establishes C *minor*, a key which prevails for several bars before the music settles onto a long trill.

With a preliminary hiccup, the violin returns to the original theme which has been almost forgotten. Full-throated, the orchestra agrees, ushered in by a rapid scale in contrary motion from the piano which was possibly executed as a glissando. (Such pianistic tricks were not unknown at the time.)

From this point onwards the music pursues a familiar course. Example TCk is revisited as is the passage which seemed so nearly like a cadenza for the three soloists. We also find the passage in which they amusingly seemed to doubt where Beethoven had taken them to. This time it takes them somewhat surprisingly to Example TCm and a series of scale-like passages which culminate in three swift ascents from cello, piano and violin in turn.

For a moment we are held in suspense until, in apparent impatience, Beethoven indicates a change to a quicker tempo. It is established by the violinist with repeated G's which seem to echo the amusing way in which the cellist had initiated the movement originally. A frantic series of variations on the rondo-theme ensues, the players seeming to want to outdo each other in virtuosity. The orchestra in a forceful *tutti* seems to be heading for E flat major but it is not to be. Back to C major we go as helter-skelter the soloists begin another 'nearly-cadenza'. This ultimately concludes with all three trilling at length on the dominant. Sobriety returns as the rondo-theme appears once more at the initial speed, almost as though the players were admitting things had got a little out of hand. Example TCj makes a farewell reappearance confirming that it is to be regarded as more important than the other subsidiary themes.

Then in a final sixteen bars that frankly find Beethoven seemingly obsessed with establishing a Tonic which in all honesty he has never left for long, the movement comes to a positive, absolute, unmistakable *end*. It is this type of overemphasis that lays Beethoven only too open to parody and perhaps is another reason for the work's neglect. There are a tremendous number of notes to be written down in a Triple Concerto and it may be that Beethoven simply tired of the project and became less than his normally critical self. If the work is perceived to have some weaknesses it is a pity, for it abounds in good themes. I wonder if the Archduke appreciated them.

Were it to wear a less exalted name upon the title-page it would no doubt be rated higher in the critics' estimation than it usually is; for Beethoven it was a case perhaps of *reculer pour mieux sauter*, a step on the way to greater things, for greater things were to follow, of that there can be no doubt at all.

Note

1. Anton Schindler, *Beethoven as I Knew Him*, English trans. 1966.
2. Emily Anderson, *The Letters of Beethoven*, Vol. 1, p. 181, Macmillan, 1961.
3. The key of A flat major seems to have been one that had especially inspirational qualities for Beethoven; a number of works in this key show this – the slow movement of the *Pathétique Sonata* (Op. 13), the comparable movement in the First Piano Concerto (Op. 15), the meltingly beautiful theme of the Op. 26 sonata variations, and of course the first movement of Op. 110.